Lisa Joanne Gilbert can usually be found standing in a field, squinting into the distance, wondering where Humbug has escaped to! She's more comfortable in wellies than in heels; the interior of her car is filled with an impressive assortment of hay, dog-hair, headcollars and chocolate bar wrappers, and if you're wondering where her bruises are from—look no further than the small, fuzzy pony hiding behind the nearest tractor!

For Humbug, without whom there would be hardly any story—but considerably fewer bruises!

And for my now grown children; Sam, Katie and Annie.

Sharing the thrills and spills as you navigated your early years to become the adults you now are, has been a pleasure and a privilege.

I wouldn't have missed it for the world!

Lisa Joanne Gilbert

WATCH OUT, HE BITES!

To Neve

lots of love,

Humbug and Toby!

(and Lisa!)

xx

AUSTIN MACAULEY PUBLISHERS®

LONDON * CAMBRIDGE * NEW YORK * SHARJAH

Copyright © Lisa Joanne Gilbert 2025

The right of Lisa Joanne Gilbert to be identified as author of this work has been asserted by the author in accordance with sections 77 and 78 of the Copyright, Designs and Patents Act 1988.

All rights reserved. No part of this publication may be reproduced, stored in a retrieval system, or transmitted in any form or by any means, electronic, mechanical, photocopying, recording, or otherwise, without the prior permission of the publishers.

Any person who commits any unauthorised act in relation to this publication may be liable to criminal prosecution and civil claims for damages.

All of the events in this memoir are true to the best of author's memory. The views expressed in this memoir are solely those of the author.

A CIP catalogue record for this title is available from the British Library.

ISBN 9781035887972 (Paperback)
ISBN 9781035887989 (Hardback)
ISBN 9781035887996 (ePub e-book)

www.austinmacauley.com

First Published 2025
Austin Macauley Publishers Ltd®
1 Canada Square
Canary Wharf
London
E14 5AA

Thanks to everyone who, over the years, has said, "You should write a book about that pony!" You know who you are, and I hope you laugh as much at the written words as you did when I told you the stories.

To our horses; Spirit, Rio, Taz, Tiff, Humbug and Toby— endless love and respect.

To Humbug's 'X' and Instagram followers, thank you all for showing me that I'm not the only crazy lady being the thumbs behind animal accounts, and for proving that there was enough interest in a fuzzy little pony to make this book a possibility.

Finally, thanks to Austin Macauley Publishers Ltd®, for taking a chance on a first-time writer, and turning her into an author!

Table of Contents

1

How It All Began

The air of heaven is that which blows between
a horse's ears.
Arabian proverb

As a child, I would have walked to the ends of the earth for
even just a sniff of a horse. I rode riding school ponies from
an early age, and when I was 12, my parents and I moved to a
rural village on the outskirts of Sheffield, and it finally
became possible for me to have my own pony!

I feverishly read the local newspaper every night
analysing listing after listing in the classifieds section, but
adverts for suitable ponies that came within my meagre
budget seemed to be few and far between. My parents had

agreed to put some money in the pot, but as it had been decided that it would fall to them to pay for board and lodgings for said pony, it seemed greedy of me to ask for much more.

In order, therefore, to save up the funds for my new equine bestie, I'd taken on a milk-round in the village (I really should go back and apologise to most of the families on my round, they were delivered of the wrong order more often than I'm willing to admit to! In my defence, I was 12 years old and I was expected to be up and about by 4 am!).

I'd worked Saturdays in a local hardware shop (having firstly convinced the owner I was 14), relieving customers of cash for items I assured them were exactly what they needed for whatever project they were undertaking (without knowing what on earth I was talking about!). I also looked after a local family's mixed collection of ducks; shutting them in each night before Mr Fox made his evening prowls.

Added to this were several years' worth of Christmas and birthday presents; I'd asked for money for the 'Pony Fund' for as long as I could remember, and my huge, bright yellow china pig was stuffed to the snout with pound notes! All in all, it amounted to just over £200! A huge amount to a pony-mad 12-year-old...not so huge when one tried exchanging it for a pony!

Eventually, one day in the spring of 1978, an advert in the paper caught my eye: '14.2hh grey mare, 4 years old, recently broken, good-natured, quick sale needed...£350 ono'. I persuaded my parents and a horsey friend that we needed to go and look before this perfect pony was snapped up by someone far less deserving, and after some sincere promises to pay back my parents for the extra cost (which I'm fairly sure I never did), I was the proud owner of an almost feral, barely-handled but very pretty Arabian x New Forest mare, who went by the unfortunate name of Thumbelina!

The name was very quickly changed, which was not something I would normally advocate, but I simply couldn't face walking into a field and shouting that! And it later became clear that what the advert meant by 'recently broken' was that the owners had put a saddle somewhere approximately within the vicinity of this pony. Undeterred, I arranged for my brand-new shiny steed to live on the farm from where my milk-round was run, and my father arranged to borrow a horse trailer to collect her.

A few days later, a completely clueless posse composed of my unhorsey parents, an unhorsey friend of theirs, and the previous owner's unhorsey father all tried some very unhorsey ways (most of which are probably best forgotten) to load the pony into the trailer. Hours later, the poor animal took pity on the incompetent gaggle of humans, and in an effort to put a halt to the ridiculous debacle, she rolled her pretty eyes and stepped daintily into the trailer. Little did she know, she was in for a white-knuckle ride to her new home, as shortly after setting off, the brakes on the trailer spectacularly failed! The weight of a loaded trailer on a very steep Derbyshire hillside pushed my dad's old blue Volvo down the hill, across the crossroads at the bottom, and into the garden of a café, where it finally came to rest against a picnic bench, scattering a number of horrified ramblers, who moments earlier had been quietly enjoying their ploughman's lunches!

I borrowed a too-big bridle from a friend and tied knots in the cheek pieces to make it fit, but it took another year before I could afford a saddle. I'm ashamed to admit that despite riding an almost feral pony bareback, with a badly fitting bridle, it hardly ever occurred to me that I really should wear a riding hat. I was now 13, and as every teenager knows, at that age you are not only invincible, but immortal too! Thankfully, I'm still here to tell the tale.

I'd named my pony Tiffany, which soon became abbreviated to Tiff, and looking back, I see that she was the stuff legends are made of. She was beautiful and almost Bambi-like to look at! Dapple-grey, with impossibly slim legs, huge dark eyes, and flutter-worthy eyelashes. She would arch her neck, toss her silky mane, flick her shapely toes, and prance delicately just for the fun of it. I received envious glances from my friends on their hefty, hairy cobs, some of which were jokingly dubbed 'a dope on a rope'.

She never really liked being ridden in traffic and would weave around like a little wriggly worm so cars had to give her a very wide berth. However, in woodland or open countryside, she was fantastic—jumping logs, fences, gates into forbidden open fields, and loved nothing more than a good, long gallop. My friend Lou had bought a lovely skewbald mare not long after I bought Tiff, but soon discovered she was already in foal.

While we awaited the exciting arrival of the 'Get One Free' part of this BOGOF deal, we would both jump aboard Tiff, one behind the other and head off into the hills for the day with a few sandwiches and biscuits in a plastic bag tied to the front of the newly purchased second-hand saddle. Happy days.

Lou and I decided the following summer that we 'needed' a set of brightly coloured show jumps if we were to be real horse owners and set about repurposing some old bits of wood, paint, and what turned out to be masonry nails that were lying around in her dad's garage. We drew plans, we measured, we inexpertly sawed, we slopped paint around, we convinced each other that we knew what we were doing, and discovered that actually, we were quite handy with a hammer…until we tried to lift our masterpieces.

We'd nailed our jumps to the garage floor! Eventually, my elderly retired grandfather, who'd been a joiner in his working life, took pity on us and made us a set of jump wings, but we lacked the poles to jump over. No problem; a neighbour was throwing out some drainpipes after a building project and we pleaded with him to let us have them. Perfect, we thought! Until a slight breeze blew the drainpipes off our brand-new sparkly jumps!

Undefeated, we made the best of things, carrying everything into the field and wedging the now brightly painted drainpipes between the two wings. We jumped our jumps, putting them higher and higher, as you do when you're in your teens and don't know any better until one of the ponies knocked the drainpipe with a front hoof and smashed the brittle plastic to smithereens!

I kept Tiff until I was 19 or 20, but found that work commitments made looking after her too difficult. At this point, she went on to give another little girl who lived in the village much fun and enjoyment. Parting with her was so, so difficult and I vowed to not put myself through the heartbreak again. I remained horse-free for a few years, during which time I married and had my three children.

It seemed very natural to paint pastel-coloured ponies around the walls of the nursery room, I cross-stitched an unfortunately gormless-looking pony to hang on the wall, bought a rocking horse for my children to ride, and spent sunny afternoons driving through the Derbyshire countryside where I excitedly pointed out horses and ponies to my small people.

My old friend, Lou, whose horse had had the foal in our youth, now had a lovely heavyweight show cob on loan from a lady who didn't have time to ride, and I confess, I dug out my old dusty boots and tried them on to see if they still fit, 'just in case' she needed help to exercise 'Mr Magoo' now and again!

Now that I was older, a little wiser, and had children of my own, I began to hope that they too would have an interest in horses and riding. I had an idyllic image of a kind, well-behaved, well-mannered family pony that would stick his pretty head through the kitchen window, gaze lovingly at us with beautiful deep brown eyes, politely hoping for an apple, while the family, sitting at the breakfast table, would laugh indulgently and congratulate themselves on sharing their lives with the perfect pony.

Ok, maybe this is an unrealistically sweet picture, but even I could never have imagined how far removed from this image real life would be!

I struggle to remember family life before the days of Humbug, but I suspect it was clean, relaxed, and bruise-free. And probably fairly boring! Humbug barged his way into our lives on 29 April 2006. He brought with him fun, laughter, frustration, and, as mentioned, a lot of bruises!

My daughter, Katie, is a middle child, with an older brother, Sam, and a younger sister, Annie. Katie was, and still is, horse-mad and has been since she was just a tot. She'd pestered for a pony of her own 'just a little one that'd live in the garden' since she was old enough to talk, and she 'talked ponies' prolifically! She'd read every pony book going; for a long time, her favourites were the 'Sheltie' books by Peter Clover, in which a sweet, well-behaved Shetland pony embarks upon adventures and generally saves the day—kind of like Lassie with hooves.

When Katie was 5, I inadvertently fuelled her desire for the horsey life by impulse-buying the horse I'd started riding occasionally, which at the time belonged to a friend of mine. Spirit was a 15.2hh Arabian x Thoroughbred chestnut mare, 5 years old at the time, but she was far too big and temperamental for Katie to enjoy, thus she upped the pleas for 'just a little one…' etc., etc.

Whizz forward several years, during which every story Katie wrote in school somehow managed to feature a pony of some description, every game involved someone role-playing a horse, and every book she read was a horsey one; by now, she'd progressed from 'Sheltie' to 'Heartland' where teenage humans, aided naturally by their equine companions, again heroically saved the day. Every family outing was interspersed with visits to various horse shows and gymkhanas, and Sunday pub lunches out with friends often included a detour to pass fields of horses.

At this point, Katie had just turned 12, was petite for her age, and was clearly still pony-mad. She was progressing well at the local riding school, riding ponies of a variety of shapes, sizes, and temperaments; had enjoyed a couple of 'gymkhana days' and always wanted to turn up early so she could groom and tack up whichever pony was allocated to her for the half-hour lesson.

I made the rash announcement, half joking, that if she helped me to look after Spirit for a winter (i.e., mucking out a cold, smelly stable, bringing in a hungry, wet horse from the field in driving wind and rain, managing rugs, feeds, hay, etc.) and afterwards still wanted a pony, I'd 'think about it' (which as we all know, is parent-speak for 'probably not'). I'd become a single parent a couple of years earlier and finances were very tight, so I needed to ensure she was as keen as she'd led me to believe. The last thing I could afford was a redundant pony eating its way through my bank balance while Katie moved on to other pursuits.

She did herself proud and as that winter turned eventually to spring, I realised that she was far more dedicated than I'd ever thought possible. Spirit was happy and well looked after; feeds were made, haynets filled, the stable clean and the yard swept, and so I half-heartedly discussed with my friend, Fran, who lived on the farm where Spirit was kept, that I might, possibly, maybe consider taking on a small, elderly pony; something quiet, kind, and preferably advertised as 'a mother's dream'.

During this conversation, Fran's phone rang. Someone Fran knew wondered if she could think of anyone who would buy her 7-year-old black and white Shetland pony.

2
Meeting the Beast

Tell a gelding, discuss with a mare, if it's a pony, then pray!
Author unknown

We'd arranged a viewing of the pony the following Saturday morning, and Fran and I set off with Katie vibrating with excitement in the back of the car. It was a beautiful sunny spring day, with the promise of a long hot summer in the air. What we had all failed to detect in the air at that point was that this was, in fact, a pivotal day, and our lives would be changing in so many ways from that morning on.

Conversation was a little stilted in the car as we all had our own thoughts about buying suitable child-friendly ponies and the benefits and pitfalls that come with them.

All the horsey wisdom warns against impulsively buying the first horse you see and we patiently explained this to Katie; advising that in order to get some perspective and a better idea of what an owner wants or doesn't want in their new equine companion, various ones have to be seen and judged against each other before finally deciding on 'the one', which ideally has all the positive attributes of the collection, and none of the negative. She nodded along to this sage lecture but clearly wasn't listening to our words of wisdom; she was far too excited!

And so it was on that bright, warm spring morning, with birdsong and an air of excitement on the breeze, that we followed the directions we'd scribbled down on the back of an old envelope (these were the days before Sat-Nav systems). Just half an hour later, we were puzzled when, after a few twists and turns, the road turned into a rutted track that disappeared between dusty builder's yards and broken down, long neglected allotments.

A few nettles and weeds provided the only greenery we could see and I was convinced we were at the wrong place... But then, we saw a dilapidated garden shed that'd had the door sawn horizontally in half, thus turning it into a small stable. A couple of scrawny chickens were scratching around in what had once been grass, and beyond them, we spotted a tiny, muddy paddock surrounded by low fencing held together with orange baler twine; a sure sign of a pony nearby!

As we parked the car, we could see a small field beyond the paddock, alongside which cars and lorries thundered up and down the M1 motorway.

Our first sight of Humbug took my breath away…and not in a good way! He looked like the result of several horses that had been chopped up and put back together by a comedian. His head was huge, his legs short, his knees knobbly, his body round and worryingly tank-like. His fuzzy mane stood up on end, his tail looked like a toilet brush, and to top things off his typically shaggy Shetland coat had been completely shaved off, and the hair was growing back in random tufts.

Add to that the fact that he immediately tried to bite each one of us, and you get some idea of his unique charm. It wasn't a promising start! Fran and I looked at each other in dismay, and then at Katie… And I realised she'd fallen in love for the very first time.

The seller was a tough-looking, weather-beaten woman called Stacey, who I'm sure had spotted straight away that Katie was smitten. Still, she delivered a very professional sales pitch, mainly I think for the benefit of Fran and me as I suspect she could see we weren't convinced of the wisdom of taking home this bizarre creature! During her impressive, non-stop monologue, she produced a driving harness, which she expertly wrestled Humbug into.

She jabbered animatedly about what a 'character' Humbug was, while deftly dodging his teeth, which were doing a fine job of snapping at whichever bit of her came within range. She then shoved him between the shafts of a little red cart, and suddenly, before us was a ready-made ride-and-drive pony! What fun! We all had a try at driving

Humbug around the little paddock and field he lived in and laughed happily about the fun Katie could have with him.

None of us had driven a pony and cart before, and I admit to visualising the enjoyment this could provide. He was then stripped of the harness and a saddle and bridle were brought out. The teeth marks in the saddle should have been a warning, as should the very small, filthy, ripped and patched-up turn-out rug that'd been almost hidden in the stable, but again, Humbug was wrestled into tack, and within minutes Katie was on board, confidently trotting around with a huge smile on her face, even popping a small jump as they tootled happily around the little field amongst daisies and butterflies.

The owner was keen to demonstrate how much Humbug loved jumping and took him riderless to the bottom of the field where a number of homemade jumps were set up. She let him go, still tacked up in saddle and bridle, and we watched in amusement as he flew with great enthusiasm around the course, stirrups and reins flying behind him, expertly clearing every jump! I still wasn't totally convinced (I'd seen those teeth!) and, as diplomatically as I could, suggested that we maybe carry on looking.

However, it was becoming blatantly clear that, in fact, Katie and Humbug were 'meant to be' and that separating them wasn't going to be easy. Somehow Humbug seemed just as smitten with Katie as she was with him; he gazed adoringly at her, hardly taking his eyes off her and he 'chatted' along with Katie in grunty little 'hmmphs' as she and I spoke about the responsibility, the time, the dedication, schoolwork, exams, blah blah blah…

It was clear that no matter what I said, the decision was already made and all that remained was to hand over a wad of

Katie's hard-saved cash and sort out the transport arrangements.

Stacey kindly agreed to 'throw in' the saddle, the made-to-measure leather driving harness, a rug, and even the little red cart for the price she was asking for the pony, and she even offered to transport him in her trailer for us (did I sense desperation?). Katie, however, was convinced she'd got a great deal. We drove the few miles home and stopped on the way at a pleasant country pub. I sat opposite Fran, with a very excited Katie chattering away at the side of me about the fun she and Humbug would have together.

In something of a daze, we ordered some much-needed drinks and pub lunches, and as they arrived at the table, I barely even noticed; on a loop inside my head screamed the words 'What the hell just happened?'.

Poor Katie had an agonisingly long week to wait before Humbug came to live at the farm; however, just to add to the excitement, during that week we were persuaded by a couple of friends that due to his diminutive build, Humbug might need a pal of a similar size to play with in case he was bullied by the bigger horses already there. Why do I listen to these people? Humbug is no more likely to be bullied than to sprout wings and fly, but at the time, we weren't yet fully aware of his unique personality, and I fell head-first into the emotional trap.

Phone calls were made to a number of local animal sanctuaries, and finally, after a couple of false starts (one pony had ringworm, another needed long-term medication), we arranged, in exchange for a large bag of cat biscuits, for a small rescue pony to join Humbug as his very own companion. Katie was beside herself with excitement and on the Big Day had prepared a stable fit for a king (or two!). Deep bedding, fresh water, sweet hay, and tasty carrots all awaited Humbug's arrival and that of his as-yet-unseen pal.

Finally, a scruffy cattle trailer rumbled down the drive, towed by an equally shabby Land Rover. Katie's excitement was at fever pitch and as we opened the ramp of the trailer, Humbug fell out! He landed with a thud in an untidy heap and a cloud of dust at Katie's feet. It turned out that he'd untied his headcollar on the journey, wandered around inside the trailer and was facing sideways, but with his bum wedged against the door! His ability to untie knots, we didn't yet realise, would be just one of the many quirks that we are constantly amused, frustrated, and irritated by.

At almost the same moment, a huge, shiny professional-looking horse-transporter attempted the tricky turn at the top of the drive, gave up, and drove down the hill into the village. Fran and I looked at each other, with that 'surely not' face, but within minutes, presumably having turned around on a wider road, the monster lorry was back. My heartbeat quickened and I felt beads of nervous sweat on my brow…

Maybe the sanctuary had misunderstood me and I'd inadvertently requested a Shire horse, or a Clydesdale, or a 17hh ex-racehorse, or an elephant; at least a couple of which I knew the sanctuary was trying to rehome. I thought about the very small stable that'd been prepared for Humbug and his rapidly approaching pal and looked back again at the enormous lorry carefully making its way ever closer. How massive was the beast that needed such a vehicle?

In the yard, the taciturn driver, wearing a grubby, sweat-stained vest, and with an equally grubby, moist cigarette hanging from his lips, dismissively pushed some crumpled, tea-stained paperwork at me, pointed at where I needed to sign, and lumbered to the back of the lorry to begin lowering the ramp. I peered nervously inside the vehicle as he disappeared into the depths, opening the numerous partitions as he went.

Finally, after what seemed like forever, he arrived at the very front of the lorry, where, tied to the side by his leadrope, was a tiny, hairy, ginger pony! The guy led the pony out, wordlessly handed me the lead rope, held out a massive paw for the signed paperwork, and climbed back up into the cab.

"Wait, what's his name?" I called. The man shrugged his shoulders, smirked, and without bothering to remove the cigarette, uttered the first and only word we'd heard from him. "Tiny?"

As the lorry reversed back the way it'd come, the pony peered shyly through his shaggy-look strawberry-blonde fringe, spotted my youngest daughter, Annie, who at the time would've been 9, and set off purposefully towards her, clearly claiming her as his own.

"Toby," she decided…and Toby he became.

3
Early Days

*Every pony deserves at least once in their life to be loved by
a little girl.*
Author unknown

The initial weeks with Humbug could only be described as
painful. He bites. A lot. Not that he's aggressive, quite the
opposite, but we can only assume that he was never taught
that biting holes in your friends was not acceptable in polite
society! It's a habit we've tried every trick in the book to put
a stop to, including, in desperation, throwing the book at him!
To no avail. Other horse owners had all given their own
suggestions as to how this habit could be stopped.

One memorable suggestion was that we carry with us one of those little plastic fruit-shaped bottles filled with concentrated lemon juice. We were told to give Humbug a swift squirt whenever he tried to bite, thus giving him a taste of sour lemons which would surely put him off biting... Needless to say, Humbug loved the taste and tried to steal the plastic lemon from us so that he could slurp up the whole lot!

Similar ridiculous suggestions have all failed, and over the years, we've become very skilled at dodging Humbug's assaults without even thinking about it. We're expert hip-swivellers, so he can't get legs and bums, arm-raisers so he can't get hands and fingers, and we've learned the hard way never, ever, to kiss him on the nose!

Naturally, Katie wanted to introduce Humbug to her school friends, and I wonder now what went through the minds of their parents when I warned that their precious offspring may be returned home with bits missing! I always tried to give Katie time and space to enjoy her pony with her friends, but one memorable day sticks in my mind, when Katie's pal, Rosa, came running into the yard where I was grooming Spirit, shouting, "Humbug's been rude with Katie and he's pushed her over!"

I really didn't know what to expect as I went down the farm track to find them, but Rosa was absolutely right— Humbug had indeed attempted to show Katie just how much he loved her and she'd buckled under his weight! She was a little tear-stained and muddied; he had a triumphant look on his face, and judging by the way he was strutting, he clearly thought he was 'The Man'! He's continued ever since to show his affection for Katie in this way, but as she's got older, wiser and taller, she's learned to simply brush him off like she would a rampant poodle.

There was once a time when, as Katie was growing leggier, I wished Humbug was a little bigger, 15hh or so, in order to prolong his usefulness. However, having witnessed him 'humping' her on too many occasions, I thank my lucky stars that he's no bigger than 8hh!

(A horse's height is measured to the 'withers' or shoulders, in hh or 'hands high' and a 'hand' is 4", thus at 8hh, Humbug is 32" high at his withers, Toby is 7hh, so 28".)

As often happens in the lives of little girls, Katie and her sister, Annie, were asked to be bridesmaids, twice within the same year, for a couple of aunties. They were delighted and went along excitedly for dress fittings, hair-stylings, rehearsals, etc. At the fittings, each bride-to-be looked in dismay at the big purple bruises flowering on Katie's arms and legs, and very quietly, she was taken to one side for serious questions to be asked.

Thankfully, Katie cheerfully explained that she'd been 'Humbugged' and sighs of relief were heard! I was always very aware that whenever my children went to places where they might have bare arms or legs on show, doubts were raised as to my parenting! Anyway, both brides banned the girls from going anywhere near Humbug for the month before each wedding to ensure he didn't bite and bruise either of them. Katie found this difficult; Humbug found it torturous!

He's always loved Katie with unparalleled passion and he simply couldn't cope with not showing that love in his own unique, inappropriate way.

4

A Taste of Freedom

Live like someone left the gate open!
Author unknown

Humbug has always been something of an escapologist. Not necessarily because he's super-intelligent and works out how to undo closed doors, gates, and fences, but rather that he's a thug and barges *through* closed doors, gates, and fences. I don't think he'd been with us a full 24 hours the first time he escaped, inadvertently aided by my then 14-year-old son, Sam, who didn't quite manage to close the stable door in time. Humbug and his new partner in crime, Toby, suddenly found themselves free, with a hundred or so acres of grass to eat and play around in.

Toby clearly hadn't paid much attention to Humbug's escape plan and was easily rounded up, but Humbug found a whole range of farm machinery to hide amongst. As Katie went one way around a tractor, Humbug's whiskery little face peered out mischievously from the other side and he ran, flicking his tail and squealing in excitement until he spotted a harvester to hide behind, and so his game continued! After half an hour or so, we humans grew tired of being outsmarted and outrun by 8hh of fuzz, and a bucket of carrots was called for. This was his downfall.

Humbug's weakness (apart from Katie) is food and, as his figure will testify, he simply can't say no.

He's gone on over the years to hatch more and more elaborate escape plans, one of which involved galloping down the hill at 'bringing-in' time, perfectly timing his escape as the owners of his full-size mates were opening the gate to take their horses out of the field. He'd apply the brakes at the very last minute, power-slide under the bigger horses' bellies, and be out through the gate before the owner of said horse realised what was happening!

He's had considerable success with this and newcomers always had to be warned. Generally, new people laughed politely, secretly thinking 'I'm sure they're exaggerating', only to later find themselves looking in dismay at the bum-end of a black and white ball of fluff as it hurtled triumphantly into the distance, kicking up its heels in joy!

I'd regularly get phone calls from various owners while I was at work, apologising profusely for letting Humbug escape but admitting that they now couldn't catch him. At the time, I worked maybe 4 or 5 miles from the farm, so I'd make a quick apology to amused colleagues (and a somewhat less-amused manager) and shoot off in the car. I always kept a couple of headcollars and leadropes in the boot of the car for such eventualities and they were put to use much too regularly.

On one occasion, during her 6th form years, Katie was at home 'studying', so after a quick phone call with instructions to get out of bed and be ready to be picked up in the next 10 minutes, we drove to the farm desperately hoping Humbug wasn't playing Chicken out on the roads. As we drove up the hill, we could see him in a field, happily munching, up to his knees in the long, lush grass that was supposed to be left ungrazed in order to make hay for the winter.

I pulled in on the roadside and Katie jumped out of the car, grabbed a tangle of headcollars and ropes from the boot, and deftly jumped over the dry-stone wall into the field. Humbug was delighted at her unexpected visit, and he whinnied as best he could with a mouthful of long grass and trotted over to her. Toby curiously was also in this field; I found out later that the lady who'd phoned me to let me know Humbug was out had put Toby in with him to keep him company!

As soon as he saw us, Toby accepted that his time in the All-You-Can-Eat-Buffet was up and began stoically making his way to the gate. I turned the car into the farm drive, just as Humbug decided to chase Toby away from the gateway. We watched in dismay as Toby galloped all the way to the bottom of the steep field and then stood snorting and stamping his tiny hoof, refusing to be persuaded back up again! Katie knew she had a long walk down the hill (and a longer one back up!) and after slipping on the headcollar, held out Humbug's rope to me.

"Erm…I'm driving the car…"

DISCLAIMER: DON'T TRY THIS AT HOME! No, really…DON'T!

He'll be fine, she said. He'll walk alongside, she said. I wound down the window and cautiously took hold of the rope, doubtful that this was one of Katie's better ideas. Humbug had arranged a carefully angelic expression on his evil little face and as I held one end of the rope in my right hand, left hand steering the car, I started to freewheel very slowly down the drive, Humbug walking quietly alongside. All went well for approximately 5 seconds, by which time the novelty seemed to wear off for Humbug.

He bucked, reared, kicked and cavorted as I, helpless in my car, stubbornly clutching the end of his rope admonished him soundly! In desperation, and thinking of the preservation of my car, I let go of his leadrope, hoping he'd make his way back to where Katie was now doubled over in laughter, leaning on the stone wall for support as she watched Humbug systematically annihilate my car! The beast was now free but still, his assault continued!

I engaged gear and steered as quickly as I safely could away from him, but as I looked in the rear-view mirror, I could see that he was running after me, neck stretched out, teeth bared; his mission clearly not yet complete! Desperately, I speeded up but he rose to the challenge and cantered down the drive after me! Eventually, after chasing me '1970s-Benny-Hill-style' around the barns, he spotted Katie (still laughing hysterically, and his distraction gave me the escape I needed.

What a nightmare! My poor car, dented and scratched, and rather curiously, sporting slobber marks bejewelled with lumps of revoltingly wet, chewed grass which were slowly slithering down the windows and wing mirrors… It suddenly dawned on me that Humbug had probably seen his own reflection in the dark-tinted windows and mirrors and was trying to rescue the poor pony that was trapped inside the car! Or eat it!

5

Happy Memories

A pony is a childhood dream. A horse is an adult treasure.
Rebecca Carroll

Summer days are often said to be longer and sunnier when you're a child, and I consider myself so very privileged to have shared happy summers with my children and their ponies. At the time I was working as a Teaching Assistant in the wonderful primary school that my children have all attended, which meant—joy of joys—6 weeks of summer holidays every year! One bright summer's day, the kids and I were sitting outside Spirit's stable enjoying the warm weather and appreciating the fresh air.

Humbug was tied securely to a metal ring attached to the wall for such purpose. He'd tried half-heartedly a couple of times to undo himself but was clearly feeling as mellow as the rest of us and gave up easily. Fran's lovely mum, Glenda, brought out a tray of orange juice and biscuits for the kids, and as she had a few minutes before leaving for her job at a smart department store in town, she sat with us on a handily placed bale of hay.

After stealing most of the biscuits and knocking over the orange juice, Humbug manoeuvred himself so he had his backside facing Glenda and looked around at her expectantly.

"What's he doing?" Glenda asked.

"He wants his bum scratching," we informed her.

She laughed and indulged him by giving him a good scratch with her manicured fingernails on the top of his little round derriere. He loved it and his top lip wiggled in appreciation as we laughed at his ecstatic expression. Slowly, he backed further and further into the source of his enjoyment and, suddenly, we realised he was sat squarely in Glenda's lap! His hind feet were completely off the floor, folded forward like a sizeable dog, as he enjoyed Glenda's scratching of all those hard-to-reach places up and down his back!

Once we'd stopped laughing, and Humbug was reluctantly persuaded to stand on his own four feet again, we released Glenda, who wasn't too happy that her smart work trousers were liberally covered in black and white horse hairs and her fingernails were filthy.

This farm holds special memories for my now-grown children. They remember long summers of picnics in the fields, building dens in the woods and dams in the rivers, making precarious tyre swings which hung high in the ancient trees, fishing for tadpoles, rescuing 'beached' fledgling swallows from the barns, cuddling litters of puppies and kittens, watching wide-eyed as calves were born, making elaborate forts in the hay (and being yelled at for it by the farmer!), and generally having an idyllic country upbringing.

Of course, Humbug and Toby featured highly in all of these activities, and even if Humbug wasn't invited along, he'd listen out for Katie's voice amongst those of the other kids and 'hmmph' back to her constantly. He'd often take matters into his own hooves if he could see her and simply barge his way through fences and over walls in order to get to her and share in the fun. Picnics are a great source of excitement for Humbug, and occasionally, I'd hear several of Katie's friends screaming as he gate-crashed their al fresco lunch!

He has rudely interrupted unsuspecting ramblers in similar ways too. One family unwisely chose to enjoy their picnic in a sunny corner of what they must have thought was an empty field. We tried to warn them by shouting as we saw Humbug spy them, but he's like a missile when food is involved, and we saw him spot them, lock on, and gallop towards the sausage rolls and scotch eggs with pinpoint accuracy. The still unsuspecting family simply waved back cheerily as we tried to make them aware by pointing and shouting…

Suddenly, their demeanour changed and panic set in! Humbug was upon them! I have no idea how much of their lovingly prepared lunch he ate; I suspect there was very little left—he's not known for sharing and I've never known him refuse anything!

This same field has a footpath along its top edge, which is used regularly by the public. For many years, the local secondary school has used this path for its athletics team to run along as part of their cross-country training. Humbug considered this to be a great idea, surely devised purely for his entertainment. He'd graze quietly in the field but keep a close eye on the comings and goings of dog walkers, ramblers, and the like.

However, as soon as the athletics team appeared, he'd set off like a rabid Jack Russell, ensuring the team could run really, really fast! The PE teacher has been seen flapping his arms, class registers, leaflets, and flags at Humbug, hoping to scare him away; if only people understood how much this excites him!

This particular farm was, and still is, a working beef farm; a very rustic place with steep, sloping fields and fences that were originally intended to keep cattle contained. Each field has a row of barbed wire running along the top of its fence, a constant concern to horse owners but which our horses thankfully respected. A couple of the fields have a natural stream running through them and most have ancient oak and horse chestnut trees around the perimeter providing shelter from the occasional hot sun or more typically, the driving rain.

When you come up the steep hill from the nearest village, there is a sharp right-hand turn off the road which leads onto the farm track to take you between fields on each side and down a gently curving slope. From the top of the track, if you look to your right, the whole of the village can be seen at the bottom of the valley. A patchwork of fields leads the eye towards woods and further farmland, dotted with grazing sheep and cattle.

In summer, the fields are lush and green, and horses can be seen grazing peacefully, swishing their tails against the flies. Each field can be accessed from another by gates and, occasionally, a couple of black Aberdeen Angus cows can be seen amongst the horses, having pushed their way through to tastier-looking grazing. More often, Humbug would be spotted amongst the cows, having done the same. As you round the bend at the bottom of the track, the view becomes more 'working farm', as does the aroma.

The large barns have corrugated metal sheets protecting the inside from the weather, stacks of hay bales are stored for winter feeding, and a variety of tractors, harvesters, and pick-up trucks are strewn apparently haphazardly between the barn and the yard. The yard itself leads to the farmhouse and has further barns built at right angles to the house, one on each side, inside which are several stables.

The beams in the stable rooves provide safe summer homes for swallows and these always caused a pleasant nuisance as they swooped through the doors, only very narrowly missing the heads of both human and horse! We got into the habit of leaving handfuls of horse hair around after we'd had a grooming session and the birds would line their nests with it, presumably making a comfy bed for the babies. The birds were very territorial and protective of their nesting sites and it was very entertaining to watch the swallows dive-bombing the farm cats.

The elderly cats half-heartedly attempted to catch the birds as they swooped at crazy speeds just slightly above the feline heads, just out of reach of paws and claws, twisting and turning acrobatically in the air as they loudly admonished the cats for daring to be around! After just a few weeks, tiny 'cheeps' could be heard from the nests and the parents frantically fed and fed and fed hungry, demanding mouths.

Before we knew it, the babies were fully feathered and standing up on the edges of the nests, sometimes five or six in each, all jostling their brothers and sisters in their determination to get the tastiest meal from their long-suffering, hardworking parents. As the babies fledged, they would often become caught in the window recesses of the stables. They'd flap frantically as they tried to fly in the open air, with the windowpane halting their progress.

They were usually easy to catch once we'd cornered them in the window ledge and we'd cradle them gently in both hands before releasing them at the door, watching as they swooped joyfully away! There was one who was presumably too exhausted to fly straight away and as Katie opened her hands after rescuing him from the window, he didn't bother to take to the skies but instead clung on to her finger with tiny claws. He sat for a while as he and Katie regarded each other with interest.

Katie shook her hand very slightly to encourage him to leave but he just clung harder! Katie grinned at me and we discussed whether he'd be carried around with her as she went off to ride (rather like a hawk on the arm of a hunter many years ago!) but, suddenly, he'd regained his breath and was off, swooping and diving as he flew. I often worried about any baby swallows that got caught in Humbug's stable window as the frantic flapping drew his attention to them and he tried to eat them on more than one occasion.

An event on the farm looked forward to with much anticipation, by not only my children but also by many others, was the annual Easter Egg Hunt! Each spring, Glenda would produce a vast Easter feast for friends and family, in true farmhouse style. The huge antique oak table would disappear under an array of tempting appetisers, several enormous home-reared roast meats, tureens of fresh vegetables, potatoes of many guises, and desserts (oh, the desserts!) to die for.

Each guest would contribute something delicious towards the meal, so as the party grew, the meal became larger and larger. Adults who arrived without children were despatched early in the day to hide an outrageous quantity of chocolate eggs around the farm. As the years went on and the children became more adventurous, eggs were hidden in ever more inventive, challenging, and potentially inaccessible spots— including one year, an egg that was hung by a length of orange baler twine to one of the bull's horns!

Thankfully, 'Paddy' was a placid beast and was more curious than furious, but even so, it momentarily stopped the children in their sugar-fuelled tracks when confronted with the sight of a massive black Aberdeen Angus bull adorned with what looked like a dangly chocolate earring!

The adults enjoyed hiding the eggs just as much as the children loved finding them, and the shiny, coloured foil-wrapped eggs could be spotted in the barn within the stack of hay bales, peeping out from abandoned birds' nests on the tops of beams, in the many nooks and crannies of the ancient stonework of the various buildings, on the just-out-of-reach branches of trees, and balanced precariously on the tops of fence posts. For the smaller and less adventurous hunters, a few were hidden in the long grass and perched on the tops of molehills in the fields.

After Humbug's first Easter with us, we realised that he had to be locked securely in his stable while the egg hunt was underway. That first year, the sight and sound of a frenzied pack of excited children running around was just too much for him to cope with and he took it upon himself to join in. Upon hearing several children screaming, the gathered adults halted as one in their food preparation, looked at each other across the table, and simultaneously uttered just a single word: 'Humbug!'.

With the help of several adults, a bucket of food and a few tasty carrots, he was eventually captured. Children were complaining, 'But he's already eaten loads of our eggs'.

Surely not, I thought, but the following morning, his 'overnight deposits' confirmed the youngsters' tale. I often wonder if Humbug is the only pony who, after a successful Easter Egg Hunt, produces poo in individual colourful, perfectly foil-wrapped nuggets!

Much later that year, Christmas approached and the holly bushes in Humbug's favourite field flourished. It might have been something to do with the copious amounts of good fertiliser they were treated to, or maybe we'd simply never noticed them before, but either way, this particular year they were abundant with glossy red berries and looked spectacular!

One day, a battered blue Transit Van rumbled down the track and the driver, a weather-beaten-looking man, explained to the farmer that he was a market trader and set about negotiating to cut some of the berry-festooned boughs in order to make wreaths that he could sell in local Christmas markets and fairs. The farmer was happy enough with this arrangement and left the guy to it before setting off on his trusty, rusty tractor to muck out his barns. The market man took off his coat, donned overalls, fished a ladder out of the back of his old van, and set to with his shears and secateurs.

Of course, this didn't escape Humbug's notice and he moseyed on over for a look. Many hours later, the farm received a phone call from a worried-sounding lady, asking if anyone knew where her husband was. He'd not arrived home at the usual time and as far as she knew, our farm was the last place he'd been, collecting holly. Suspicions hadn't yet pointed at Humbug having a hoof in the man's mysterious disappearance and the farmer pulled on his boots to go and have a look.

The van was still parked in a little clearing not far from the yard, a long-cold flask of coffee, a couple of sandwiches, and a mobile phone blinking with many unanswered messages all sat forlornly on the seat. The farmer wandered up and down the track, hoping to gain some clues as to the disappearance of the man, hoping he'd not fallen and broken his neck! Finally, the farmer spotted a ladder lying in the grass and went over for a closer look.

Suddenly, he heard shouting from the top of an enormous holly bush and looked up to see the market trader frantically waving. The farmer leaned the ladder against the bush, held it steady, and helped the now very cold, hungry man to climb down. A brief conversation was had, during which it became clear that Humbug had found the ladder leaning against the bush and had leaned on it to scratch his neck; his head had gone through the rungs and off he'd walked, wearing the ladder like a rather rigid scarf!

Unfortunately, this rendered the market trader helpless and there he sat, high up in the boughs of the prickly holly bush, trying not to move for fear of being spiked, hoping someone would come along to rescue him! Humbug by this time had rid himself of the ladder but apparently paid regular visits to the bush to make sure his new pal was still there. The market trader told the farmer that he didn't realise ponies could grin in such a wicked way! Funnily enough, he didn't bother coming back to cut the holly boughs he'd not managed to collect on his first visit!

6
Fun and Games

Feeling down? Saddle up!
Author unknown

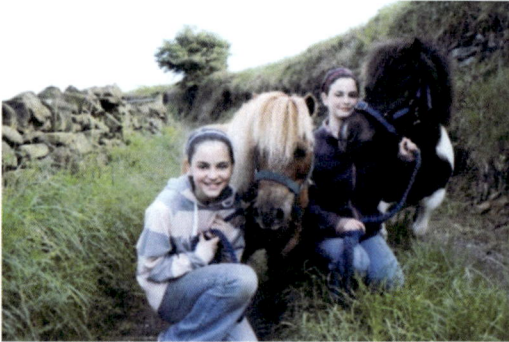

We quickly came to realise that Humbug is at his happiest when he has a job to do, such as going out pulling the cart, or being ridden along the lanes on a pleasant hack. He likes being busy and enjoys being made to feel important. However, getting him ready for riding or driving has never been without serious risk of being bitten.

One summer, we even resorted to putting a muzzle on him just so that we could tack him up. Having never driven a pony before, we initially had little idea of how the complicated-looking harness fits together, and trying to work out which bit goes where and then fit it all onto an impatient, fidgeting pony that seemed to have teeth everywhere was definitely a challenge! The trick is for one person to keep his teeth occupied, preferably with a tasty mineral lick, pony nuts or small bits of carrot, while someone else quickly and efficiently fits the harness.

This approach is time-limited, as Humbug's attention span is like that of a gnat—he gets bored incredibly quickly and looks for trouble (usually with his teeth). However, once he's tacked up and ready, he's well-behaved and enjoys his outing.

Of course, if riding him is the intention, actually getting aboard Humbug is often a challenge in itself. He has always been happy to be ridden but getting him to that point usually proves tricky. He knows every tacking-up diversion in the book, including biting, stamping, barging, escaping…the list is endless. If you're not really quick fastening up the girth, the saddle often ends up on the floor as he rubs it against the wall, or he'll dip one shoulder so it simply slides off.

Once you've reached underneath a fidgeting, thrashing, kicking pony to grab the buckle-end of the girth, while holding the saddle in place with the other hand, actually buckling up the straps seems like such an achievement, to the point where you feel like riding the beast is secondary to everything that's gone on before! Once buckled up, the challenge is to clamber aboard really quickly before he bites.

Biting is his last-ditch attempt to divert from the riding plan and he puts extra effort in, snapping at whichever bit of you is nearest, combining it with stamping on unsuspecting toes, squashing you against walls, and then when the already exhausted rider is just at the point of putting weight in the stirrup, he lets out the breath he's been holding since the girth was buckled up, thus becoming several inches thinner... The saddle and the half-aboard rider have often ended up underneath him, while he smiles malevolently, having achieved his goal!

Katie and Annie found that as they were getting taller, they could hop aboard Humbug as they brought him in from the field and could ride him bareback to the yard. The first time they did this, it puzzled him greatly, as suddenly he was being ridden without having had the fun of objecting. He thought about things for a while and realised that if he shook himself, rather like a large wet dog, it was extremely difficult for the girls to stay balanced, and they'd often end up in a laughing heap on the floor!

They've both become accomplished riders having learned to second-guess what Humbug would do to prevent them from staying aboard; valuable lessons in horsemanship.

We discovered early on that Humbug's a 'sensationalist'. He's excited by loud noises, bright colours, strong flavours, and lots of activity. Katie had a few scary moments in the early days when she realised that while out riding if Humbug is passed by a noisy motorbike, he can't help himself but chase it! What he'd do if he ever caught one I dread to think but this is just another one of his many quirks. He did a similar thing once when I'd gone out for a pleasant summer hack around the quiet country lanes on Spirit.

Katie had also come along riding Humbug and was a few feet behind. A very noisy car with a 'boy racer' exhaust approached from behind us. Spirit flicked her ears back nervously and I felt her become quite tense; even though I felt sure she wouldn't shy, I patted her neck to reassure her. At that moment, I became aware of some excited squeals from behind us and the clatter of Humbug's little hooves approaching at speed as he attempted to get a head-start on racing with the noisy car! Katie was struggling to hold him back and I reached down and grabbed a hold of his reins just as he and the car went past, its driver clearly wondering what kind of circus act he'd stumbled across!

Similarly, Humbug loves thunderstorms and the fireworks on bonfire night; the louder, the better! While the rest of the local horses are sedated by the vet, listening to soothing channels on the radio and snuggled up in their cosy stables by anxious owners, Humbug is out in the field, his neck and head stretched skywards, watching the lightning or the bright colours of the fireworks and trotting around excitedly as he anticipates the next loud bang!

We owners tended to move the horses from one field to another throughout the year; as one became over-grazed they'd all move to another one while the first one recovered and so on. Humbug's favourite field on this farm was very steep, had lots of hiding opportunities in the shape of trees and bushes, had natural springs flowing through it, perfect for paddling and splashing fun, and it had a deep cleft through the middle, as though millions of years ago the field had been folded in half like a sheet of newspaper and then opened up again.

Humbug would play happily in this field; it's the one with the footpath running along the top of it which provided him with the prospect of chasing unsuspecting dog walkers, ramblers, and athletics teams! In later years, a flock of squawking chickens scratched around in this field too, and on dark rainy nights, it was the best field for avoiding capture. One of the best features of this field for Humbug, though, is the fact that from the gateway, he could watch tractors being repaired in the farm's garage.

Machinery on working farms seems to require a lot of maintenance and much of that maintenance seems to involve loud revving engines, lots of shouting and swearing, the dropping (or throwing) of large metal tools, and a radio blaring out loud rock music. All very exciting for a small hairy pony who loves noise! He'd mill about around the gate while the fixing was going on and watch intently as tractors and harvesters were manoeuvred over the servicing pit.

Thankfully, the pit was securely covered by a huge sheet of thick metal once the repairs had been finished for the night. Most of the horses avoided stepping on this sheet as they didn't like the hollow sound it made; not Humbug. At bringing-in time, Humbug would make a special effort to walk across the metal, stamping each of his little hooves to ensure he made as much noise as possible!

Once he'd walked the length of the sheet and his feet were once again on terra-firma, he'd often spin around and drag along whoever was leading him back along the metal just so he could have the pleasure of hearing himself stamp along it again!

7

A Mind of His Own

There are only two emotions that belong in the saddle; one is a sense of humour and the other is patience.
John Lyons

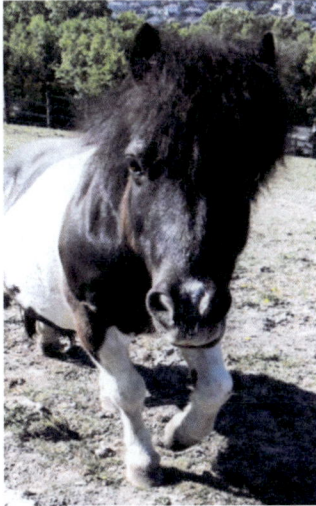

For all his fuzzy cuteness, Humbug hasn't been easy to live with. He's a bully and a thug, totally obnoxious and immensely greedy. If, in his opinion, the grass in another field looked tastier than that in his field, he'd happily barge through fences, gates, walls, and barbed wire to get into it. Once there, he'd realise the grass was actually no better or worse, so he'd come back through the wall, fence, etc., but not necessarily through the gap he'd already made, thus causing further damage for which we had to apologise.

For many years, we used electric fencing to make a paddock in an attempt to keep him contained. On many occasions, we've been convinced the battery pack was faulty as invariably Humbug would be found on the 'wrong' side of the paddock; however, when any of us were brave enough to touch the fencing, it was working just fine as our stood-on-end hairstyles testified! Eventually, we realised he simply doesn't care that he gets a shock from the fence and climbs through it anyway.

Either that or his hair was just too thick for him to feel the 'tickle'. A rather sadistic friend suggested shaving his chest (Humbug's, not his own!) so that his almost bare skin got a shock as soon as he leaned on the fence. This we did, with some very small feelings of guilt, but although the resulting shock caused Humbug to raise his eyebrows slightly, it still didn't dissuade him from his escapology pursuits.

We've realised over the years that nothing short of a bear-pit would keep him where we want him, and he'd have a try at scrambling out of that too, so we try not to stress too much about him. As already mentioned, he's ridiculously greedy and we're confident that whenever he escapes, he'll generally head towards where he thinks food is, so we've always made sure he knows where the feed store is, but we keep it securely locked!

For the first few years, when Katie was small enough to ride him regularly, she really struggled with Humbug's forceful personality. They clashed on a number of occasions when they were out riding; Katie would want to go one way, Humbug the other. Considering Humbug's strength and stubbornness, Katie didn't stand a chance and often found herself being taken along roads, through local parks, and up garden paths with little choice in the matter.

Humbug, however, always enjoyed his outings, but Katie found she often had to apologise for his behaviour. One day, he spotted an elderly lady walking along the pavement towards him. She'd obviously been shopping and had a carrier bag of groceries in each hand. This excited Humbug greatly, as not only did she potentially have food but she didn't have a free hand with which to bat him away!

Moments later, as bananas, toilet rolls, and tins of beans littered the pavement, a red-faced Katie apologised profusely for Humbug's misdemeanour, and Humbug, satisfied that he'd not missed anything, trotted away happily, unaware, or unconcerned at the hassle he'd caused. During the same outing, he spotted a chap washing his car by the side of the road. Presumably thirsty from sampling all those toilet rolls, Humbug helped himself to a soapy drink from the wash bucket.

The chap, around the other side of the car at the time, shouted a cheery 'Good morning' to Katie as she struggled to drag Humbug's head up and out of the water. She often wonders what he thought when, on returning to wash out his sponge, the chap found his bucket completely dry! Any child (or indeed adult) walking along the pavement with an ice cream was in serious danger of being mugged, or at the very least finding a slobbery lick-mark down their lolly!

An outdoor school provides a great means of keeping horses and ponies fit and exercised during the long winter months when riding out on the roads after school or work is impossible. Unfortunately, Humbug thought being ridden in the school was immensely boring. He therefore found ways to amuse himself; these included galloping full pelt across the school and skidding to an abrupt halt while lowering his head, flinging Katie at speed over his ears. He'd then stamp on her fingers and run away, snorting in glee as she lay spread-eagled in the sand, a mouth full of dirt and with her bruised fingers throbbing. He also learned that he could lean against the fence as he walked around the perimeter, causing Katie to lift up the leg on the fence side to avoid it being crushed against the posts. As he felt her weight distribution change, he'd skip either forwards or sideways, knowing she was unbalanced, and often leave her in mid-air, crashing to the ground as he trotted away across the school, tail whisking happily!

Another trick he perfected was to grab at the tasty-looking leaves that poked temptingly through the fence from the trees on the other side. On one occasion, he got more than he bargained for and the whole branch broke as he dragged the leaves through. Unwilling to let go of his bounty, he trailed the branch with him, happily munching on the tasty greenery. However, the branch got caught between his front legs and he tripped over it, fell, and squashed Katie beneath him. I watched this happen, heart in my mouth from the other side of the school.

It's amazing how disasters happen in slow motion in the observer's eyes, and as I saw him crash to the floor, crushing my small, delicate, immensely breakable daughter beneath him, I set off running towards them, already thinking of how

I'd explain it to the paramedics that would be called upon to patch Katie up. Humbug was visibly horrified and, as soon as he sorted out his limbs from the offending branch, he scrambled up, immediately looking down at Katie to see if she was ok.

She was fine, thankfully, despite being a little winded, and as she reached up to help herself to her feet using Humbug's considerable shaggy mane, his attention wandered and he realised he'd let go of his leaves. He stepped sideways to grab a mouthful and Katie lost her grip, falling yet again into the dirt!

8

The Chaperone

*A horse doesn't care how much you know until he knows
how much you care.*
Pat Parelli

As a single parent of now teenage children, it would've been
easy for me to worry about the girls becoming too interested
in boys with fast cars. With Humbug in our lives, I had no
such worries. Humbug clearly assumes he's the only man
worthy of Katie's attention and feels that he's the only one
allowed to get suggestive with her. He's the benchmark
against which all of Katie's potential boyfriends have been
measured and if they didn't love her as much as Humbug

does, then they were not considered worthy of her attention or affection!

One boyfriend in particular, quite promising for a while, tried for Katie's benefit to enjoy the whole horsey thing, but it soon became clear that actually he wasn't keen. One day, the boyfriend decided he'd been at the farm long enough, thought of somewhere else he had to be, and opened Humbug's stable door to make his impatience known to Katie. As quick as a fat, fuzzy flash, Humbug made his break for freedom, not caring that the boyfriend was still standing in the doorway.

Said boyfriend found himself with the front end of a Shetland pony between his legs, and suddenly as his feet left the ground, he found himself being carried along at speed as he clung by his teeth to Humbug's rump! Five minutes later, after being unceremoniously dumped in the dirt by Humbug, I realised his days were numbered; he looked sulkily at us girls rolling on the floor laughing and announced that he'd never liked horses and didn't want to come to see them anymore!

As I'm sure you've come to realise, Humbug makes his opinions very clear, and where Katie is concerned, we know that no human is ever likely to be good enough. He has always been insanely jealous of anyone being even near Katie, as I've found to my peril. There was once an occasion when Katie and I were walking together in the horses' field. Katie was upset about something or other and I put my arm around her. Big mistake!

I felt a huge thump between my shoulder blades, and as I staggered forwards, arms flailing as I desperately tried to stay on my feet, I realised Humbug had taken exception to my comforting Katie and had reared, punching me in the back with his front hooves! Even though we'd got to know Humbug very well over several years at this point, I was still shocked by the level of his jealousy and aggression. I made a point of trying to chase him away, thus asserting my dominance over him. This didn't go down well!

He was furious and came at me with his whole arsenal of weaponry—back hooves, teeth, body barging, front hooves, teeth again… It went on and on for what seemed like hours, but I felt the need to let him know that his behaviour was unacceptable and that I should be allowed near my own daughter. I kept pushing him away, waving my arms, shouting, but he just kept on coming.

It became clear after a time that neither of us was going to win this battle and, eventually, we looked into each other's eyes; panting, battle-worn gladiators—and silently acknowledged that we understood each other. A truce had been called that day and I felt a slight shift in our relationship. Even so, I rarely turn my back on Humbug, and woe betide anyone who tries to harm Katie while Humbug is around!

9
Necessary Tasks

Our perfect companions never have fewer than four feet.
Author unknown

HUMBUG & TOBY

During the life of a male horse, there comes a time (or several times if you're a dedicated owner and so inclined) when, as an important part of the grooming regimen, the 'boy bits' have to be cleaned. This involves long rubber gloves and a ready-made solution that comes in a handy squirty bottle, enabling the solution to be dispensed from a distance.

This is essential for us; bearing in mind the shortness of Humbug's legs, the cleaner would otherwise need to be bent double and be very much underneath a randy Shetland, who gets a huge buzz from having his tackle fiddled with! The cleaning solution is dispensed from the sexy, sleek, black bottle with instructions suggesting it's washed off with warm water. We've discovered, the hard way, that having warm water 'there' is just too enjoyable for him and he spreads his back legs wide, half closes his eyes, and emits a low 'mmmm' noise! Quite nerve-racking for whichever person drew the short straw and is underneath him fiddling around with his manhood! Cold water, we've discovered, is the way to ensure his mind is elsewhere.

Responsible horse owners protect their equine friends from internal parasites by way of ready-prepared worming medicine usually dispensed in syringe-like tubes. Many horses, including my lovely mare Spirit, aren't keen on the taste of these, despite them being labelled as 'apple-flavoured', or 'minty', or whatever. It's often a battle to position the tube in an unwilling horse's mouth and keep it there while you squeeze the plunger in order to deliver the measured amount of paste onto the back of the tongue, thus ensuring the horse has little choice but to swallow it.

It can be done quickly and efficiently and is over in seconds, but still, Spirit would back herself into the corner of the stable when she spotted me coming so armed, and would lift her head high enough so that I'd be looking up at the underneath of her chin, while she concentrated on rolling her eyes, clamping her lips closed, and generally being a drama queen! Humbug, on the other hand, loves being wormed. He's terribly excited by the whole process and, over the years, has developed the ability to suck the paste from the tube!

Due to his and Toby's diminutive size, one standard tube of wormer can be shared between the two of them. We've learned to administer Toby's portion first, otherwise Humbug slurps up the whole thing before we can stop him! Because he's so enthusiastic, he tends to grab the tube in an effort to steal it, rather like a dog being teased with a chew toy. He has bitten through several tubes and they're not flimsy.

I tried once, in the name of research, to cut through a tube with a big pair of scissors; it took a lot of doing, which shows the strength of Humbug's bite (the bruises on my legs testify to this!). He licks his lips after he's been dosed to ensure he's got every little bit, but by doing so, often spreads remnants of paste around his mouth and nose. This he'll wipe on the nearest handy human, but will then realise what he's done and lick it back up again so as not to waste a single morsel.

In more recent years, scientist boffins have discovered that horses don't actually need worming quite as often as originally thought, so testing kits are available. This revelation has seen horse owners throughout the country donning rubber gloves, poking bits of steamy horse poo into very small plastic pots, and then placing the whole thing inside a flimsy envelope, and posting it to the lab for analysis! I do often wonder what the postman thinks!

The trouble is, unless we see Humbug and Toby actually lifting their tails and depositing a pile, it's impossible to know whose is whose. The whole stable often looks as though someone has sprinkled a box of raisins across it. And you can absolutely guarantee that they refuse to perform while they're being watched! Funnily enough, as soon as you turn your back to exchange pleasantries with another owner, the tell-tale 'plop' can be heard, but by the time you turn back, there's no knowing who produced which of the two steaming piles that have magically appeared.

I'm not aware of many individuals who actually enjoy having work done by a dentist (myself definitely included!). Humbug, of course, is the exception. The 6-monthly check-up is viewed by most horses as, at best, an ordeal, but Humbug eagerly anticipates his turn, eyes wide, feet stamping impatiently as he watches his pals being coaxed and cajoled into having their teeth checked and filed, seemingly looking forward to his turn. However, we've realised he simply looks forward to it as an opportunity to bully and bite someone new!

The dentist turns up with a van full of scary-looking equipment, designed I'm sure to make wimps like me go wobbly from the knees up. One essential piece of equipment is the 'dental gag', which is like a bridle but it has metal plates that fit between the horses' teeth that can be cranked open in order for the dentist to insert his whole arm into the horse's mouth without fear of it being crunched.

He'll often offer part way through fiddling around in there to let us put our own hand in to feel the 'before' and 'after' states of our horses' teeth, including Humbug's, and while I nod along and make all the right 'Oh yes, I see' noises, actually, all I'm thinking is how Humbug will find some way of paying me back for the indignity of me inserting an arm and messing around with his gnashers!

Now, it has to be said, that the dentist we used at the time is a big bloke! He's easily 6'6" with blonde curly hair, an angelic rosy-cheeked expression and he's built like a barn, so a stroppy 8hh Shetland is simply not going to faze him. In fact, the first time he encountered Humbug standing up on his back legs and punching with his front, the dentist never even broke eye contact with us, let alone halted in his conversation, and he simply caught Humbug by a foreleg mid-rear and held him there!

Humbug's face was an absolute picture; never before had he been challenged in this way and he was flummoxed. The dentist continued to support Humbug's weight, while at the same time talking to Katie about how thousands of years ago, before dentists were needed to poke around up to their elbows in a horse's mouth, equine teeth were kept in tip-top condition quite naturally by the harsh, scrubby, rough grass they ate.

Ironically, we horse owners now spend time, money, and effort to produce soft, lush grazing that does absolutely nothing to keep the teeth worn down and smooth but which contributes to liberally lining the dentist's pockets with a lucrative income.

Eventually, he turned his attention to Humbug, lowering his front legs gently to the floor. Humbug thought about things for a moment before rearing again, although with a little less conviction this time.

"Fine, have it your way," the dentist laughed, and again caught one of his forelegs, holding it so that Humbug was completely upright while, with his free hand, he deftly slipped on the gag bridle and quickly cranked open the mechanism which opened Humbug's mouth wide. From this position, the dentist could see using the bright beam from his head torch right to the very back of Humbug's mouth. After scooping out some soggy, half-chewed grass, which no doubt was being saved for later, it was decided that a 'quick rasp round' would keep Humbug smiling like a film star until the next check-up.

Now, the 'quick rasp round' is the bit that most horses hate, but which Humbug loves! It fulfils his need for sensation; predictably he seems to enjoy the noise of the file as it rattles and vibrates across his teeth and around his head and he'll stand willingly on all four hooves for this to be done. Once his teeth are filed and smooth, the dentist runs his hand across all the surfaces to ensure no sharp points can protrude into his tongue or cheeks, he then uses an enormous metal syringe to squirt minty mouthwash around all the hard-to-reach places and wash away the debris.

Naturally, Humbug thinks this is a splendid idea, and once relieved of the gag, he tries his usual trick of sucking the mouthwash from the syringe. In actual fact, there is no need for Humbug to suck up the minty freshness, as low and behold, there's a bucketful of it right by his feet! All of the dentist rasps and files and whatnot are, in fact, attached to the inside of the bucket by clever little hooks and all of them have their 'business end' below the surface of the minty solution, thus making a visit from the dentist a tasty one for our horses.

I'm surprised it took Humbug as long as it did to notice the bucket, but once he did, it took three of us to drag his head out of it to stop him from drinking the whole thing!

After dealing with Humbug, I suspect the dentist assumed he could stand upright, stretch and ease all the knots and kinks from his spine. Then we brought out Toby, who at 7hh, is even smaller! The dentist let out a sigh of resignation and we saw his shoulders momentarily sag. He then took off his jacket, folded it neatly, and placed it carefully on the floor. He must have seen our puzzled expressions as he smiled, winked, and sat down on his jacket.

He took hold of Toby's leadrope and manoeuvred him so that he was straddled across the dentist's outstretched legs. Toby seemed a little bemused but it meant that the dentist could work on his teeth without having to be contorted into all kinds of unnatural and uncomfortable positions. Toby predictably was as good as gold and stood patiently, accepting his fate with little more than raised eyebrows when the rasp was being wielded. The dentist explained that even though Toby is so very tiny, he still has the same amount of teeth, of a very similar size, to those of a much larger horse.

He told us that mini-Shetlands often have dental issues because of this, but thankfully, he declared Toby's teeth to be fine and dandy.

I discovered on one of his more recent visits that what I assumed were horse treats (sugar-free, of course!) rattling around in his coat pocket were actually teeth removed from various equine heads and kept for the purpose of educating his clients on the care and health of their horses' mouths. Fascinating in his opinion; grizzly in mine!

10
Road Trips

Equestrians walk a fine line between bravery and insanity...and a few of us use that line as a jump rope!
Author unknown

Humbug, for all his stubborn, obnoxious bloody-mindedness, is a great nanny for nervous or anxious horses. He has often been borrowed by friends to accompany their horses and ponies on journeys to vets and such like, as he loves a road trip in a horsebox, but is well-known for causing havoc wherever he goes. Humbug was once called upon for this very purpose when his pal, Murray, had to visit the vet for some investigations.

Murray is owned by a friend of Katie's, so the two ponies knew each other well and travelled happily together in a trailer borrowed from another friend. On arrival at the vet, it was decided to leave Humbug in the trailer while Murray was undergoing his examinations. Humbug, predictably, had other ideas, and while the vets were doing their thing, a loud thumping and crashing could be heard as Humbug attempted to disassemble the trailer! It became clear that he was getting out of there one way or another, so Katie went to release him.

Once out, he went and stood quietly and calmly with his now sedated friend and offered him the moral support that he felt he needed.

As time went on, and Katie grew taller, it became less comfortable for her to regularly ride Humbug. After some searching, she bought herself a beautiful dapple-grey 15.3hh thoroughbred mare. Despite a thorough (and expensive) vetting before purchase, Rio was diagnosed with navicular syndrome not long after she arrived and during diagnosis, travelled to the vet on a number of occasions for investigation and treatment.

On seeing the rather posh lorry we'd hired for the first visit, Humbug's eyes grew wide, and even though Rio travelled well on her own, we didn't have the heart to leave the little guy at home. We loaded him and Rio up, tied their leadropes to the tie-rings, and jokingly wondered where Humbug would be by the time we arrived.

Needless to say, during the half-hour journey, he untied himself and not only had he turned round so he was facing backwards and not forwards as the lorry was so arranged, but he'd somehow got out of his own partition and was squashed inside Rio's half with her! The lorry had a 'groom's door' just behind the driving cab giving access from outside to the horse area without having to lower the ramp. We opened this to check on them as soon as we arrived and Humbug leapt happily out.

His headcollar and leadrope were dangling forlornly from the ring we'd tied him to, so he was quickly rugby-tackled by Katie, who clung on with her arms locked around his neck until his headcollar was released and he was again restrained! While Rio was being examined, x-rayed, nerve-blocked, etc., Humbug was locked into a stable which overlooked the examination area (we'd learned from the previous trip with Murray that Humbug doesn't like to be left out, and besides, the lorry was a very expensive one and to replace it would have cost me a fortune had he destroyed it).

He made eyes at several of the vet-nurses and they were drawn to his fuzzy cuteness, going over to fuss and stroke him. He fooled them easily into believing he was sweet and cuddly. However, several utterances of "ouch" later, we knew they'd learned the hard way to leave him alone! Realising he'd lost his audience, he reared up so his front feet were over the half-door, leaned over and expertly unlatched the lock with his teeth, thus letting himself out.

Several people were standing around the now sedated Rio but he trotted straight over to Katie, who was upset at the result of the x-rays, and he tried to comfort her in the only way he knew—biting her on the leg!

11

Outgrown

Horse riding is the only sport where your equipment can decide not to cooperate with you.

Author unknown

Difficult conversations were very briefly had as to what we would do with Humbug now that Katie, rapidly approaching adulthood, had a horse of a more suitable size to ride. The sensible thing to do when a pony is outgrown by its small jockey is to advertise it for sale and do your best to ensure it finds a lovely home to carry on its career as another child's best friend.

However, we had doubts as to whether it was morally ethical to pass on our fuzz-covered devil-spawn to a poor unsuspecting family, knowing he'd cause them some serious nightmares and bite holes in their children! In any case, Katie was utterly horrified at the prospect of selling him on and we did wonder how Humbug would have coped without Katie in his life. I realised with a sinking heart that it looked like we'd got him...for...ever!

We were concerned that now that Katie had Rio to ride, Humbug would simply vegetate, grow fatter, and become depressed from lack of work, so a naïve plan was hatched where he could be led from Rio occasionally when Katie took her out for a hack. We tried this once, and only once. Not only was Rio appalled at the idea of having Humbug lurking malevolently alongside her, but Humbug, easily bored, entertained himself by nipping at her legs and diving underneath her to get to tasty grass verges on her other side!

How he didn't strangle himself with the leadrope, or wrap it around Rio's legs and trip her over, I'll never know. We also had to be aware of Humbug's love of chasing motorbikes, and bearing in mind Rio wasn't particularly confident in traffic at this point, our plan was clearly doomed from the start.

Our plan B was that Humbug could be lunged in the outdoor school on a regular basis to give him some exercise and a sense of purpose. The idea of lunging is that the horse calmly walks or trots in a well-behaved manner in a large circle around the handler, while the handler, holding one end of a long lunge line attached to the horse's bridle, stands in the centre and pivots as the horse travels forwards.

Humbug clearly hadn't read the rule book and after completing maybe half a circle, he was already bored and ran bucking and squealing at Katie who was in the middle of what she'd hoped would be the circle. She managed to dodge him as he ran past her and reeled him in, gathering up the line and setting him off again, hoping for a full circle this time. No chance!

Humbug had discovered a distraction and not only ran at her, snapping his teeth and threatening to bite as he came alongside, but he then carried on galloping and towed her around the outdoor school, knowing full well that his strength far outweighed hers and that there was little she could do to stop him or even slow him down. We tried time and time again to lunge him, each time with pretty much the same result.

Other horse owners would stand at the school fence and offer helpful advice; however, they somehow always declined our suggestion that they put their wisdom into practice!

Although lunging Humbug in the outdoor school had spectacularly failed, something he had always enjoyed was gymkhana games! We'd set up poles for him to weave in and out of, homemade flags on long poles for Katie to reach out and grab as they galloped past them, balance beams made from milk crates and long planks of wood for Katie to run along while Humbug trotted alongside, and a couple of small jumps for him to clear.

For once, this satisfied his need for lots of activity, colour and entertainment. He and Katie, despite the fact that her feet now almost touched the floor, would race against the clock—

in and out of the poles, grab a flag, back down the poles to stick the flagpole in a bucket of sand, Katie would leap off him and mince along the balance-beam, leap back on, collect another flag, they'd gallop back to the bucket and post flag number 2, race to the jumps, clearing them in a fashion worthy of an Olympic showjumper.

They would arrive back at the start in a flurry of dust and horsehair, stirrups flying, Katie's hat askew, and huge smiles on both of their faces! We were aware that Toby was missing out on all the fun, but because of his miniature size, he has never been broken in to ride. No problem. Annie ran alongside him as he carefully weaved in and out of the poles, they collected a flag and posted it, Toby delicately trotted along while Annie negotiated the beam, they both popped over the (lowered) jumps, and arrived back at the start.

Neither Annie nor Toby seemed to embrace the fun with the same enthusiasm as Katie and Humbug and I could see that 'Thanks, but no thanks' look on Toby's furry ginger face.

Humbug's gymkhana looked so much fun that I decided Spirit and I should have a try. Humbug and Katie were racing around the school at breakneck speed, clouds of dust in their wake, and after a moment of watching, Spirit looked at me in absolute horror! Her face in that single moment conveyed a whole diatribe of 'If you think I'm going in there with that pony and playing childish games, you clearly don't know who you're dealing with'.

I cajoled her into the school and persuaded her to walk around, looking at the flapping flags, the coloured poles, and the comparatively tiny jumps. She glanced scornfully at each of these and looked across at Humbug, who was raring to go, pawing the ground, stamping and spinning in his excitement at having a worthy competitor! Spirit rolled her eyes and sighed, clearly thinking 'Ok, let's get this over with'. Annie, the adjudicator, suddenly shouted, "Ready, Steady, GO!" And Spirit and I found ourselves eating Humbug's dust!

While Humbug galloped away, eyes wide, nostrils flaring, little hairy legs going like pistons, Spirit delicately trotted through the weaving poles, snorted in alarm as I reached out for a flag, eventually allowing me to carry one at arm's length back to the sand-filled bucket and plant it there. Meanwhile, I could see from the corner of my eye that Katie and Humbug were already clearing the second and final jump!

Spirit and I cheated slightly, missing out the balance-beam, and went straight for the jumps, both of which she knocked down disdainfully before walking with a blatant lack of enthusiasm to the finishing line where the dust was starting to settle around a panting, wide-eyed, adrenaline-filled Humbug! It was clear that Spirit wasn't destined to be a gymkhana pony and the game, no doubt to her relief, was not repeated.

After several plans to exercise him, which all ended up with us being bruised and bloodied, we decided Humbug was probably fine, keeping himself fit and entertained by scrambling up and down the steep Yorkshire hills, chasing ramblers, and climbing over walls to escape into other fields. We did still drive him around the lanes occasionally and even bought another cart so that Toby could be driven too!

By this point, Katie and Annie had spent a summer breaking Toby in to drive, and it made a sweet picture to see the two ponies out and about being driven by the two girls, red 'L' plates stuck to the back of each cart, and often accompanied by a couple of their friends and usually one or two of the farm dogs. One drive we all enjoyed was just up the hill from where the horses lived. It meanders along quiet roads on a gentle incline, with fields on each side full of grazing cattle, sheep, and an abundance of birdlife.

One of my favourite birds is the Lapwing, and there are lots of them in and above the fields, wheeling and diving over our heads, seemingly for the pure enjoyment of it! There's something rather lovely about driving a pony and cart through the countryside; it's a peaceful, pleasant way to travel. The smooth rhythmic motion of the cart as it follows a willing, happy pony definitely beats driving in a stuffy car, with the windows tightly closed so the air-con can function, the countryside whizzing past and the radio blaring out the latest hits.

This particular drive took us on a 4-mile tootle (quite a long way for very short Shetland legs!), passing, at the halfway mark, the local hunt yard. Hunting horses generally see many things throughout their career which they are usually un-worried by, but they would often trot over to the wall in order to snort and stamp in alarm at Humbug as he proudly trotted purposefully past with his happy occupants sitting in the cart!

We found that while we were out driving, it was always difficult to get very far without a car stopping in order for its occupants to take photos of the ponies! We'd have the same conversation again and again on a Sunday afternoon:

"Yes, yes, they're really cute, but watch out for the black and white one; he bites!"

"…Told you so!"

12

Flipping Chickens and Woolly Mammoths

There is nothing so good for the inside of a man as the outside of a horse.
John Lubbock (although often accredited to Winston Churchill!)

Humbug and his horsey pals became used to the comings and goings of other creatures on the farm. Dogs had puppies which would then be sold on to new homes, the cat would have kittens high up in the hay barn which, once found, would also move on.

The cows are a beef herd, so although the babies can stay with their mums until they're at a natural weaning age of almost a year (this doesn't happen with a dairy herd when the babies are taken from the distraught milker mums often at just a few minutes old in order to maximise the poor mum's milk yield), eventually after another 18 months or so of eating good, muscle-building grass, they go to market to be sold on to other farms for fattening up, or to be the basis of a new herd elsewhere, later producing their own offspring.

One summer, a redundant garden shed was converted into a hen hut and a flock of feathery squawking chickens took up residence. Humbug loved the noises they made and followed them around the field, sniffing at them and watching closely as they scratched around. Humbug being Humbug, it didn't take him long to realise that as they were scratching in the dirt, beak-down, bum-up, he could stick his nose underneath them and flip them into the air!

I suspect it was the excitement of the sudden flapping and squawking that made him pursue this new hobby. Oddly, the chickens didn't seem to mind and simply regained their feet and carried on in their search for worms and bugs. Over the years, Humbug continued to enjoy the company of chickens and could often be seen dozing in the field surrounded by a dozen or so of his feathery lady friends, some of which liked to flap up and perch on his sizeable backside for a spot of sunbathing.

He did still amuse himself by flipping them occasionally, but generally, they lived alongside each other fairly amicably.

One thing Humbug doesn't like is a sheep. Even worse, several sheep! They've become known in our family as 'Daft Woollies' for obvious reasons; they're daft and they're woolly. There was a big flock living on a neighbouring farm and, occasionally, a few would pay a visit to our place; probably getting through a gap in the wall that Humbug had previously made. Anyway, Humbug would snort and stamp his front hooves in anger if he spotted them in his field; he really hates them!

There were a number that visited one misty winter's day and he behaved as though they were rampaging woolly mammoths; the look of astonished horror on his face was priceless and he positioned himself so that he was between them and Katie in order to protect her from whatever evil they were about to inflict. We wrestled Humbug into the stable, locked him in, and set about trying to round up the sheep in order to send them back through the gap in the wall, but as anyone who's tried to persuade sheep to go somewhere they don't want to go will tell you, this was easier said than done.

Sheep struggle to understand basic instructions, rarely do as you want them to do, and often don't even run in the same direction as their friends! Eventually, after getting nowhere with our marshalling skills, and with thirty or so sheep now running wildly around our field, the scruffy, taciturn shepherd was called. He turned up with several days' worth of grey stubble sprouting from his chin, lank, greasy strands of grey hair hanging limply from under his flat cap, and wearing oily, grubby trousers fastened at the waist with what was once orange baler twine.

A filthy shapeless jacket hung from his skinny frame and tough-looking sturdy boots were on his otherwise bare feet.

This bothered me far more than it should and I made a resolution to present him with a gift of comfortable, warm, woolly socks. Speaking to Glenda later, she told me he probably preferred it that way as his feet would doubtless be so tough from a life outdoors, that he'd perhaps find his crusty, roughened old skin would snag the wool. I never did provide socks!

Anyway, he brought with him an equally scruffy collie dog to round up his strays and between them, they quickly and skilfully herded the sheep onto a trailer. Just 20 minutes later, and without having said a word to any of us, he drove them back down the hill to their own farm, but Humbug patrolled the field carefully every morning for weeks afterwards to make sure it was safe.

13

Hide and Seek

There is much we can learn from a friend who happens to be a horse.

Aleksandra Layland

Even now, during his advancing years, you can never fully guarantee that Humbug, once out in the field, will be willing to be caught again. In his youth, though, there'd be times when he'd be standing at the gate demanding that he be the first one to come in, sometimes he'd be up the hill but would come thundering down when we shouted him.

This in itself has its hazards as, because of Humbug's top-heaviness (his head is disproportionately large!), he's not great at stopping once he's galloping downhill and often we'd have to dodge out of his way at the last minute before he squashed us against the gate or trampled us underfoot. More often, he'd be nowhere to be seen. We provide him with a warm, dry stable every night, deep comfy bedding, a couple of nets filled with tasty hay, a bucket of fresh water, a buddy to keep him company... What more could a pony possibly need?

But Humbug, being the bloody-minded brute that he is, would often decide, usually on a cold night in winter when the wind is howling and the rain is being driven horizontally into your face, that he wants to stay out and play for just a bit longer. He's not always easy to spot on a Yorkshire hillside in the dark; you'd assume that his white bits would show as you swung the torch beam back and forth, but Humbug's white bits are usually caked in a liberal coating of mud.

Anyway, he developed a skill for hiding—in dips, behind trees, gorse bushes, and the like—in an effort to prolong his fun! He's like a naughty child who, on being discovered during a game of hide and seek, squeals excitedly as he runs to find his next hiding place!

This could be considered quirky or charming on a warm summer's day when you're not cold, wet through to your pants, and don't have the family's meal still to prepare. An hour and 45 minutes is the longest 'game' he's played, and on that particular winter's night, not too long ago, I was alone, as both Katie and Annie, now adults, were working.

I'd already had a battle to bring Spirit and Rio in from the field as they were upset by the weather and had dragged me around as they spooked at imagined crocodiles which were surely lurking in every shadow and even, according to Rio, had climbed to the tops of the swaying trees and were threatening to drop onto her from the overhanging branches. Swear-jar-worthy words were uttered as the wind blew my hat from my head, startling the already wound-up mares as we neared the yard.

They both panicked and got away from me, leaving me standing alone on the farm track, wet, miserable, hatless, and feeling utterly defeated as they clattered noisily into the yard without me, thus announcing my apparent ineptitude to the other horse owners (whose horses, I felt sure, had walked calmly from the field alongside their owners like little angels).

When I caught up with them, I gathered up their trailing, muddy leadropes, muttered threats of glue factories and dog-food recipes and deposited them in their respective stables, whereupon they calmed down immediately and tucked happily into their suppers. Rugs were changed, feet were picked out and cleaned, haynets hung, and as I looked out of the half-door at the howling gale which was now blowing sleet against the farmhouse windows, my heart sank... I still had to find (and catch) Humbug.

I walked the short distance across the yard and back to the field, hoping against hope that Humbug's whiskery little face would be peering at me through the gate. There was indeed a whiskery little face, but it was Toby, bless him, asking very politely to be brought into the stable for his supper. Humbug, as predicted, was nowhere to be seen.

Hoping that he'd see me and feel aggrieved that he was missing out, I made a big fuss of Toby as I put on his headcollar and led him out of the gate, all the while calling Humbug's name, hoping he'd come thundering down the field at full speed, skidding to a sloppy halt in the muddy gateway, which even now he tends to enjoy doing.

After settling Toby in for the night, who I have to say was delighted at the prospect of having the bed to himself and first dibs at the haynet, I returned to the field, having resigned myself to the probability of a long search. That particular field was huge, very steep and had several natural springs flowing from various points. I had a couple of glimpses of Humbug as I shone the torch around, occasionally his eyes were picked up in the beam as he watched me through the driving rain and sleet from the tops of the hills as I searched for him. By the time I'd climbed up to wherever I'd seen him, he'd gone.

Although from time to time, I heard him as he galloped past, not quite close enough to be grabbed, I had very few actual sightings. By this time, I was even colder, wetter, hungrier, and more miserable than I'd been before I'd started playing Humbug's ridiculous game of cat and mouse.

Evil thoughts of waving him off to the glue factory drifted enticingly through my head as I climbed, slithered, and stumbled up and down the steep hills in the now pitch dark, watching as one by one the other horse owners' car headlights lit up the rain on the track far below as they drove home having tucked up their well-behaved horses for the night. I felt sure they were all going home to warm comfortable houses, each one no doubt heated by a large traditional Aga, from which delicious aromas of hearty home-cooked meals drifted.

During these musings, I trudged upwards and, holding my hat on against the blustery wind with one hand, torch clutched in the other, I carried out yet another sweep of the top part of the field, which I knew from experience was Humbug's favourite spot. At the very top of the hill, I was struggling to stay on my feet as the rain and wind howled around me when suddenly, I heard a 'hmmph' immediately behind me!

Humbug was following me, his head held low, but not in any apologetic, shamefaced way, while he considered his appalling behaviour; no, he was simply using me to shield his face from the driving rain.

You'll be pleased to know that I managed to resist the temptation to beat him with a large stick, and as I slipped on his headcollar and fastened it up, he bit me hard on the leg, just to make sure I was in no doubt as to who'd won the game!

14
Woe Is Me

A horse is a thing of such beauty...none will tire of looking at him as long as he displays himself in his splendour.
Xenophon

As Humbug has started to get older, his joints have become a little creaky. He has never minded being out in the field in all weathers and has often come into the stable at night perfectly happy but with a thick layer of snow on his back, which Katie would sweep off with the yard brush! However, in the past few years, age has definitely started to catch up with him. Shetlands are known for being an extremely tough and weatherproof breed, and they grow a thick double coat in winter. Their manes and tails are also very coarse and thick in order to provide them with extra warmth. Humbug has all of this, but due to his advancing years and his creaky joints, we still felt the need to provide him with a bit of extra warmth on very cold, wet days in the shape of a rug; particularly as each winter, we clipped most of the thick woolly fur off his neck and body to prevent him from overheating in the stable at night. Humbug looks incredibly cute in his rug and he knows it!

However, getting him into it was, and has remained a challenge. He simply hasn't got the patience to stand still and be buckled up, so he stamps, spins, barges around, kicks the door, bites Toby, bites us, spins again…all the while, a poor human is grappling with straps and buckles! We've tried tying his leadrope to the ring on the wall while we do up the rug, but this doesn't help as he amuses himself by squashing us against the wall.

Plus, he has a knack for quickly untying himself, or he'll quickly slip his ears out of his headcollar by rubbing his head along the wall, allowing it to drop to the floor, so it's simply a case of getting the rugging up done as quickly as possible. Once his rug is on, and he's outside, he's perfectly happy; he will tootle around all day in the heaviest of rain, and be perfectly warm and dry knowing he looks the 'bee's knees'!

We didn't want Toby to feel left out, so he too was provided with a rug, but because he's so tiny, every rug we tried looked like a long dress on him! As we decided on the one that was the best of the bunch, a 'foal-size' rug which was still a bit big, he looked at us with that expression on his face that you sometimes see on children whose mums say 'But you'll grow into it in no time!'. Toby puts up with such a lot; he shares a stable with Humbug, which gives you a sense of his patience and character!

Over the years, he's been dressed up in various homemade outfits, had ribbons plaited into his mane, had his tail trimmed far too short when Annie once became a little over-enthusiastic with the scissors and has had his hooves painted with sparkly polish of every colour. He takes all of this very much in his stride and will happily stand all day to be primped and primed, all the while gazing adoringly at Annie. She once taught him to 'yawn' on command and this is his party trick.

Whenever he feels he's missing out on attention, suddenly his little pink tongue sticks out, he closes his eyes, and his mouth opens wide. Naturally, we all chorus, 'Aww, good boy, Toby!', which prompts him to do it again and again! If Toby were any smaller, he'd make a perfect lap dog. He's very calm and gentle, loves attention, loves cuddles, and on summer days when we're sitting in the field enjoying the company of our horses, he's the one who'll be amongst us enjoying some quiet time with Annie.

Humbug is likely to also be there, but is more likely to be stamping on our fingers, biting our legs, and getting randy with Katie!

One early spring evening, all the horses had been brought in from the field and as we were bedding them down, we realised that something wasn't quite right with Toby. At this point, there was nothing specific, he just seemed a little out of sorts. Annie sat in the stable with him for a while and as he rested his head in her lap, she understood that actually, he was potentially really ill. As any horse owner will know, colic can come on very quickly, and depending on its severity, is often fatal.

Suddenly, Toby was groaning in pain and started to lie down in order to roll. All the wisdom at the time advised to never let a colicking horse roll as its gut could twist, thus causing a slow painful death. Annie literally lifted her pony to his feet as I grabbed a headcollar so that we could walk him around outside, thereby preventing him from rolling and hopefully prompting his bowels to move, thus relieving any potential blockage.

Oddly, Humbug had kept himself in the background as we'd paid all our attention to his pal. This is unheard of and it was only when we opened the door to get Toby outside that we realised we'd missed his barging and biting. Humbug was clearly concerned and let us out without fuss, but as we walked with Toby to the outdoor school which was around the back of the ponies' stable, Humbug went crazy.

He was whinnying, shouting at the top of his voice, and we could hear him stamping around, kicking the walls and door in his effort to know what we were doing to his friend. I felt bad for Humbug but Toby really needed all of our attention as we tried to keep him upright. It took both Annie and me to hold him up as his knees buckled; he was clearly in a lot of pain, which minute by minute was getting worse.

The emergency vet had been called and after making a note of our postcode, said he'd be 20 minutes…it felt like he said 20 hours! We struggled to keep Toby on his feet and despite his mini size, he was very heavy as he couldn't help but collapse to the ground. An hour later, the vet still hadn't arrived and we frantically kept ringing a number that simply wasn't being answered. Toby was becoming more and more exhausted from the increasing pain he was in, and Annie despite trying to be very calm, was obviously distraught.

Humbug had upped the volume and was now screaming for his pal. I can't begin to describe the relief when half an hour later, the vet rang. He apologised for the delay, apparently, he'd got hopelessly lost in an area with very poor phone signal, but as it turned out, he was now only a mile away; he'd turned up at the wrong farm. 5 minutes later, he took one look at Toby, being pretty much held up by Annie, and then looked at me with an expression that I'd dreaded seeing.

He explained that because Shetland ponies are so small, their internal organs are also tiny, thus making internal examinations almost impossible. Often a blockage or a twist in the gut of a larger pony can be rectified by the help of a vet wearing a long rubber glove, but he said in Toby's case, this wouldn't be possible. We took Toby slowly back to the stable where the vet had offered to inject muscle relaxants and painkillers in an effort to make him more comfortable while nature took its course.

He admitted that he didn't hold out much hope and suggested that we prepare ourselves for the worst, but also agreed that ponies do sometimes recover from colic even at this stage. Humbug again, although relieved to see his buddy, gave the vet some space to do what he needed. A set of clippers shaved a patch on Toby's neck so the cannula could be inserted. The needle at first didn't quite hit its mark, and bright blood stained Toby's fur, the vet's arm and the floor.

But, eventually, after a few tries, the drug was flowing into his system and he started to seem more comfortable.

The vet warned us that this was simply the effect of the painkillers and that he was still critically ill. He advised us to walk him around for 5 minutes every 20 minutes for the next few hours and basically told us he couldn't do any more, it was all up to Toby now. We stayed the night and walked Toby every 20 minutes as advised. By midnight, he was exhausted due to the pain and the stress but we carried on, trying to convince each other that he was starting to look better.

Katie arrived at 1 am, coming straight from her job as a waitress, and after a 12-hour shift, immediately took her turn to walk Toby with us. At 2 am, Glenda brought out hot chocolate, biscuits, and a couple of blankets; the temperature was below freezing and there was a heavy frost sparkling on the ground. With tears in her eyes, she gave each of us a wordless hug, patted Toby on the head, and went back inside. On and on we went, each taking turns walking Toby and becoming more and more desperate.

4 am is a desolate hour, and we felt utterly disheartened that so far, there had been no sign of improvement. Finally, at around 6.30 am, he started to show some interest in what was going on around him and there seemed to be a bit of a spring in his step. We didn't dare get too excited but he was definitely improving. An hour later, he lifted his tail and did a tiny poo, proving to us that his gut was working again, and after that, he literally perked up before our eyes! He even had a nibble at the haynet, admittedly not very enthusiastically but it showed he was feeling better.

Humbug was obviously delighted that his little pal was starting to feel better and showed his relief by biting him on

the bum! We finally allowed ourselves to breathe and relax...
It'd been a long, long night!

15

Things That Go Bump in the Night

Horses are angels with hooves, sent to Earth to teach us
about love, trust and patience.
Pam Brown

It wasn't the first night we'd spent at the farm, nor would it be the last. We invest a lot in our horses, both financially and emotionally, and if any of them look under the weather, we're prepared to stay with them night and day and do whatever needs to be done in order to make them comfortable. Katie had a few sleepless nights with her mare, Rio, who, it turned out, was a real drama queen! It seems that with even the slightest twinge of pain, she would take to her bed like a simpering lady of Victorian times, wafting herself with her fan and calling weakly for the smelling salts!

Rio had an unusual tendency to sleep if she was in pain and had us baffled on a number of occasions when we were aware that she wasn't feeling right but could do very little about it as she was stretched out in her bed, snoring like a pig! Rio too had a colicky event not long after we got her but it seemed mild and the vet simply prescribed keeping an eye on her. Katie stayed the night and has some amusing video footage that she captured on her phone of Rio dreaming…her feet were twitching rather like a sleeping dog dreaming of chasing rabbits! Bearing in mind Rio started her life as a racehorse, we wonder if she was dreaming of winning!

The farm could be an interesting place to spend a night. If you weren't frantically trying to get a horse to stop colicking, then you might notice all the strange little noises that accompany the bewitching hours. Katie and her pal, Rosa, once pestered and pestered to spend a night in the stable with the ponies. They would have been around 13 or 14 at the time; they'd heard the rumours about the farm ghost and were fascinated. Eventually, their pestering got the better of me and I gave in.

I knew that they would be safe enough at the farm, the house was within shouting distance of the stable, and anyway, Humbug was very protective of Katie and I knew he wouldn't let anyone get near her, supernatural or otherwise. I did warn them that the farm would be a very cold place at night but they wouldn't be put off, so sleeping bags were dug out of the loft, warm socks were found, a flask was filled with hot chocolate, and biscuits were stashed in excited anticipation of the midnight feast.

They lasted until about 8 pm! I got a phone call from a quiet little voice saying, "We're cold and Humbug's eaten all of our biscuits." As I drove them home to warm beds, I smiled to myself and resisted the temptation to say 'I told you so…', but I did tell them so!

The children have grown up listening with wide eyes to stories of the farm ghost, so were never particularly worried by the possibility of coming face to face with it. We'd never felt spooked by being there alone on dark nights, although over the years, we did have a few strange happenings. The first time something 'odd' occurred was one bright, warm summer's day when Katie and Annie were grooming the ponies; admittedly not the conventional time for hauntings that movie directors would have us believe!

Humbug was tied up outside the stable and Toby was inside being brushed by Annie. Annie had put one of her brushes on the partition between the stable and the storage area, roughly her shoulder height. She turned to pick it up but it was gone. Assuming Katie had taken it, she went to look but Katie was using her own set of brushes on Humbug. Annie looked around on the floor, wondering if the brush had fallen and was in the bedding, but it was nowhere to be seen.

Frustrated, she assumed again that Katie had taken it and was playing a trick. She called out, "Can I have that brush back, please?"

Suddenly, it fell from an old wooden beam high up in the rafters and landed in a flurry of ancient dust at her feet! We were absolutely speechless! There was no way any of us could've put the brush up there, it's at least 20 feet high!

When we later related this story to Fran, she simply said, "That'll be my grandad, Jack."

Oh, that's ok then!

Apparently, 'Grandad Jack' was a typical farmer of his time and had a deep love for his Shire horses with which he worked the land for many years. He was reported to be the very last farmer in the area to make the reluctant switch to mechanised farm vehicles, preferring to use horsepower. He was also known for being a lover of practical jokes, with which he amused and entertained his children, grandchildren, and great-grandchildren for many years.

There was an occasion not long after this when we were pottering around the farm, mucking out, filling haynets and doing all the horsey jobs that fill several hours of every day. Suddenly, an elderly man walked past the stable door and rounded the corner into the farm's pretty walled garden. Assuming he was a neighbouring farmer looking for the front door, I called out to him, but receiving no answer, I went after him, intending to redirect him back to the kitchen to where I knew Glenda was.

I rounded the corner and looked, puzzled, at the empty garden. There was nowhere he could have gone as the garden was bordered on all four sides by a dry-stone wall but he clearly wasn't there. I went into the kitchen and explained to Glenda that there was possibly an elderly man wandering around. She told me she'd been at the kitchen window for a while and would have seen someone in the yard, particularly if they were near the stables. We then realised that the farm dogs (there were seven of them at the time) were still all lying in a puddle of sunshine and none of them had barked.

Normally, as soon as anyone came near the yard, either on foot or in a vehicle, they were welcomed by the cacophony of six border collies and a Jack Russell, all trying to outdo each other in the decibels department! I must have looked confused, and Glenda asked me to describe the chap. Old bluey grey cap, dark blue coat, tweedy trousers, and sturdy black boots.

"Is this him?" She asked, taking a small, framed, slightly faded, black and white photo from a cabinet.

There he was; my little old man, standing with a big smile on his face, between two smart Shire horses in front of what was now Spirit's stable!

"That's Jack, he died 20 years ago," she told me.

I could now put a face to the prankster who'd dropped Annie's grooming brush at her feet, but I admit to being just a little shocked!

Grandad Jack was spotted once more, but this time, by one of the other horse owners. We were leaving the farm one night, Annie a few steps behind me, face in her mobile phone, walking towards where we'd parked the car. As I said goodnight to the other owner who was closing her stable door for the night, she asked, "Who's the old guy with Annie?"

I turned around to where Annie was walking towards me but saw only Annie! The lady went very pale and swore she'd seen an elderly man walking alongside Annie, and looking intently at something on her phone screen. By the time she'd asked the question, he'd vanished! She described an elderly man, wearing a blue cap and coat, tweed trousers, and boots!

16
On a Diet

In riding a horse, we borrow freedom.
Helen Thompson

One day, when Katie was hacking Humbug along the quiet leafy lanes, she was stopped by a crusty old farmer, leaning on his dry-stone wall, chewing thoughtfully on a piece of grass. "Tha shunt be riding that there mare while it's in foal," he declared in his best broad Yorkshire accent. Katie was mortified to explain that the 'mare' was, in fact, an overweight gelding, hence the exercise.

The farmer persuaded his creaky old bones into bending almost double so he could take a look at Humbug's undercarriage and was amazed to find 'boy stuff' instead of the expected mare's udder. He let them go on their way, apparently shaking his head in disbelief. We knew at this point that steps had to be taken to prevent Humbug from exploding.

Humbug has always shown an enthusiastic appreciation for food and as such has spent every spring on restricted grazing. Or that's been our plan, anyway! Short, fat ponies are prone to laminitis, a crippling inflammatory condition which affects the tissues (or laminae) that bond the hoof wall to the coffin bone (or pedal bone) inside the hoof. The condition can actually affect any horse or pony of any age, at any time, but small, fat, lazy ponies who tend to gorge themselves on lush spring grass are particularly susceptible.

Unless detected very early, the condition can be deadly as the coffin bone can separate from the hoof wall and rotate downwards, potentially piercing through the sole of the foot. It's an agonising condition and one we're desperate to avoid, thus the restricted grazing plan. Humbug has shown varying degrees of dissatisfaction at this plan, despite us explaining to him that it's 'for his own good'.

One way to restrict Humbug's grazing is to keep him in his stable for a large portion of the day. We've provided him with entertainment opportunities such as 'trickle-feed' balls with pony nuts, carrot sticks, and the like stuffed inside which drop out (or trickle out) as the ball is rolled around. Humbug broke the ball almost immediately, by shoulder-barging it to the floor in frustration that the food didn't trickle out quickly enough.

We then drilled holes through turnips and suspended them on long strings from the rafters hoping to keep both Humbug and Toby occupied as they tried to work out how to take a nibble from a swinging vegetable. However, working as a team, they captured the turnips in a pincer action and gobbled them up within minutes. We bought them a 'Space Hopper', which wasn't the success we'd hoped.

We'd seen a number of home videos on various social media sites of horses and ponies playing with similar toys, picking them up by the handle, throwing them around, chasing them, and generally having a jolly time. Toby, however, was terrified of it and cowered in the back of the stable, his eyes wide and a horrified look on his face! Humbug waved it around for a bit, but then predictably bit a hole in it.

Although excited by the resulting loud 'pop', he then became immediately bored by the piece of limp orange rubber lying at his feet, pawed dismissively at it with a front hoof, and looked at us with an 'Ok, so now what?' expression on his face! We were running out of ideas when a friend suggested floating a number of apples in a tub of water. Bearing in mind our plan was to reduce their food intake, I was aware that almost every entertainment option we'd tried so far involved food!

Anyway, we eventually decided to give the apple-bobbing idea a try. Humbug loved it! The tub we used was bright purple, made of sturdy plastic, and was maybe 18 inches high but perhaps 3 feet across. We filled it, and it took a lot more buckets of water than we expected, but eventually, it was ready for the hard, sour Bramley cookers we'd bought especially. We'd naïvely expected to float the apples in the water and for Humbug and Toby to spend time gently and politely 'bobbing' for them; possibly taking turns and enjoying being entertained for hours.

What actually happened was that Humbug stuck his head straight in, up to his ear-tips in water, pinned an apple to the bottom of the bucket, dug his teeth in, lifted the apple out, and gobbled it straight down! By the time we'd opened the stable door to go in and stop him, he'd done exactly the same with the other apples and Toby hadn't even had a sniff at one! Humbug, hoping we'd got more apples concealed, frisked us and checked all our pockets, but ignored us rudely when we admonished him for spoiling the game.

Then, realising no further fruit was forthcoming, he proceeded to climb into the tub of water. He had both front legs, his belly, and one back leg immersed before the whole thing split and started to collapse, flooding the stable and their bed (around £50 worth of cardboard shavings) in what surely had to be far more water than had gone in the tub in the first place! Humbug was delighted by his new impromptu indoor pool and pawed excitedly with a front hoof at the rivulets and the resulting puddles.

Toby retreated to the very back corner of the stable in an effort to keep his feet dry and watched in disgust as Humbug sunk to his knees and then rolled around in the gathering puddles, managing to coat every bit of him in what was now very dirty water!

Because our plans to entertain the ponies during their incarceration had spectacularly failed, we made the decision that we'd been trying to avoid—fitting the ponies with grazing muzzles. It meant they could go out into the field with their pals but their intake of grass would be drastically reduced. I'd been reluctant to try muzzles as I just knew that Humbug would escape from it and he'd be eating as much grass as ever.

The ponies would also look like Hannibal Lecter, which personally, I thought wasn't an attractive look! A grazing muzzle looks like a fabric bucket which fits over the horse or pony's nose and mouth and is fastened by straps behind its ears, rather like the kind of thing seen on aggressive dogs. There are strategically positioned holes which allow the pony to breathe, drink, and still graze a little, but make it tricky to guzzle large quantities of grass.

Toby resigned himself to the wearing of his muzzle, and although he did a great job of making me feel guilty by looking very sad, he accepted his fate with stoicism. Humbug, not so much! After Humbug had worn once what he clearly thought of as some medieval instrument of torture, he made it very clear that he had absolutely no intention of wearing it again. It regularly took three of us to wrestle him into the muzzle while he bit, kicked, spun, and reared in his efforts to resist it.

Once in it, he'd appear to resign himself to his fate, although as we pretty much predicted, every day at bringing-in time, Humbug would be muzzle-free, stuffed full of grass, and grinning at us wickedly. Every day we'd go looking for the missing muzzle and would find it hung on the fence, on gateposts, on low tree branches, and we once had to retrieve it from a dollop of poo, noticing that it'd been well and truly stamped in.

We mentioned this to the owners of the other horses, many of whom said they'd watched Humbug hook the headpiece on the fences and gateposts, etc., and then simply back out of it. We questioned as to why nobody had thought to put the muzzle back on him but were often told, 'This IS Humbug…!'

Fair enough. We tried putting a headcollar over the top of the muzzle but he simply removed both. Once, he very cleverly managed to remove the muzzle but kept the headcollar on! That must've been a tricky manoeuvre, particularly as we'd learned to thread one through the other, but as you'll have realised already, this is no ordinary pony! Then, there was 'The Incident with the Fence'. Along the tops of the walls around the field ran a length of strong, taut wire, which was fixed at intervals to wooden fence posts. One day, presumably while he was trying to remove the offending item of torture, Humbug somehow managed to attach the muzzle's spring clip that went underneath his chin to the wire fencing, thus rendering him captive. By the time we found him, he'd worn a path in the grass along the bottom of the wall, approximately 12 feet long, which was the distance between two posts and the only distance he could therefore walk, there and back.

He had a crick in his neck for days, where his head had been at an unnatural angle for hours on end, and some slight scuff marks on his belly, which stuck out and had rubbed on the stones which made up the wall. It has crossed my mind since that it might not have been Humbug who attached himself…maybe one of the other horse owners was taking the opportunity for revenge!

Eventually, we gave up and decided he'd have to spend more time in the stable. He had Toby for company and enjoyed having a chat with anyone who walked past the stable during the day as they went about their business. Toby was happy enough to come inside with him as he also didn't like the muzzle, but the way Toby showed his distaste was to stick his tongue through the grazing hole in the bottom!

Then, a genius friend suggested that ponies won't guzzle quite so much grass if they're inside during the day and are turned out into the field overnight. We were a little sceptical but tried this, and low and behold, it worked! Both ponies soon became used to their new routine and were often standing waiting at the gate to go to bed as soon as we arrived at silly o'clock every morning. We found that we had to turn up crazy early just in case Humbug decided he wasn't going to cooperate. We were time-limited as we all had work, college, and school to go to, so had to allow ourselves enough time for Humbug being...well, Humbug! Once caught, the ponies would go into the stable, yawn, stretch, and settle down in their beds for the day! It suited them to be out of the sun; as already mentioned, Shetlands have thick coats and although they shed the majority of the woolliness at the end of spring, they could never be described as 'sleek'!

The ancient stone walls of their stable were around 2 feet thick, so in summer, it was always pleasantly cool in there. Humbug and Toby happily slumbered away the hot hours of the day and enjoyed the cool evenings out in the field with their friends! We cautiously left off the grazing muzzles and kept a close eye on their weight, but magically, they didn't balloon, and the theory that they wouldn't guzzle overnight seemed to be true!

We did a bit of research and discovered that current thinking by the boffins was that there was less dangerous sugar in the grass overnight than during daylight hours, so it was safer for them to eat it.

One of the problems we found though with keeping the ponies in the stable during the summer days was the dust. Stables created from old farm buildings tend to have generations' worth of dust, cobwebs, birds' nests, old hay and bedding, not to mention the spiders! One summer, Humbug developed an annoying, tickly cough, which rapidly got worse.

We made sure he was out in the field when we swept the stable, we'd already switched from wood shavings to dust-free shredded cardboard for their bedding, we washed down the dusty walls regularly, and we soaked or steamed their hay, but the cough persisted. We bought a cough medicine from the local horsey shop which, predictably, Humbug loved! He'd grab the bottle as soon as we went into the stable and while we wrestled it back from him to remove the cap, he'd be virtually climbing up us to snatch it from our hands.

Imagine trying to hold a juicy bone above your head away from an excitable (and fat!) labrador dog and you'll get some idea of Humbug's determination to reach the bottle! The instructions suggested pouring a spoonful onto food or hay in case the horse or pony took a while to get used to the strong taste, but there was never any need to do this with Humbug, he was perfectly happy to drink it straight out of the bottle! The medicine worked for a while, but then, worryingly, the irritating cough came back. Or so we thought.

It took a while for us to catch on but, eventually, we realised that Humbug only 'coughed' when he saw us opening up the feed store where the medicine was kept. Without us noticing, he'd trained us into providing him with the tasty, sticky liquorice-flavoured medicine on demand! It took a while to break him of his habit and so determined he was to be medicated, that he put more and more effort into his coughing. So much so, that he developed an impressively loud cough/fart combo, which although ridiculously funny, alarmed Toby no end!

17
A Gentle Soul

Horses change lives. They give our young people confidence and self-esteem. They provide peace and tranquillity to troubled souls. They give us hope.
Toni Robinson

Despite his 'Humbugness', Humbug does have a sensitive side. It's well hidden, admittedly, but we do occasionally catch him being sweet. He loves babies. Baby anythings can be reasonably assured of being well looked after by Humbug. A friend who likes horses visited the farm one day. We'd not seen her for a while as she'd recently got married and was busy setting up her home with her new husband. Humbug was somehow not his usual self and was actually being very quiet and gentle around her.

We commented on this, puzzled by his new behaviour, and the friend confided that she'd just had her first pregnancy confirmed! Almost 2 years later, the same friend along with her little daughter came to see Spirit, Rio, and the ponies. Humbug sniffed gently at the precious toddler, bundled up in a flowery all-in-one, and surprised me by not eating her. She reached out a chubby hand and I held my breath, mentally dialling paramedics. She grabbed hold of the fleshy ridge above Humbug's nostril and chuckled. I nearly passed out!

As I squinted through one eye at what I was sure would be carnage, I saw Humbug breathing softly on the little girl's cheeks, tickling her with his whiskers, and allowing her to grab and squeeze his nose and lips; he actually seemed to be enjoying this interaction and at no point did he show the slightest inclination to inflict pain! I admit, it's not a scenario I'd be in a rush to repeat, just in case it was a fluke and he actually did eat someone's child, but for a few moments, we saw a very caring, soft side that we don't see often.

The next time we saw his sensitive side was when one of the farm dogs decided the best place to give birth to her puppies was in the ponies' stable. Border collies are well-known for their intelligence, but clearly, this one was having an off day! Maybe it was the prospect of giving birth many times over that was addling her brain, who knows, but for reasons only known to herself, Fly decided her birthing partner should be Humbug.

He rose to the challenge like a professional midwife, all but mopping the labouring mum's brow. Eventually, when the ordeal was over and there were ten healthy, squirming, squeaking black and white puppies in his hay, we gathered them up in order to move them to more suitable accommodation. He wasn't happy and muscled his way between us with an anxious expression on his face, sniffing at his adopted family, clearly worried as to what we were doing with them.

Finally, when they were settled with their exhausted mum in a quiet, empty stable, a comfy old quilt and soft bedding underneath them, we took Humbug to visit. Again, he gently sniffed each of them as they slept, carefully checking each one over until, satisfied they were in good paws, he left their mum in charge.

One summer, it was decided that one of the elderly hens should hatch a brood of chicks. We anticipated the fluffy yellow bundles with much excitement and suddenly, one day, there they were! Katie took one to show to Annie and Humbug spotted it as she walked by. Katie bent down, the tiny fluffy bundle cheeping in her hands, and Humbug sniffed gently at it. He seemed delighted and looked, eyes shining at Katie, before turning his attention back to the chick.

He blew softly through his nostrils (each one the size of the chick!) and gently ruffled the chick's fuzz; again I was terrified that he'd eat it but he was happy to gaze adoringly at it as it fell asleep safely cradled in Katie's hands.

The opposite of Humbug's sweet side is what we usually see and my youngest daughter, Annie, often seems to be on the receiving end. For some reason, Humbug occasionally takes a real dislike to her and will rear and punch at her when she goes into the field for whatever reason. Annie is a kind, gentle, quiet soul, who has never done any wrong to Humbug, but there have been times when she has been on duty that she's had to phone Katie or me to ask for help as Humbug simply won't cooperate.

There was once an occasion when Annie was bringing both Humbug and Toby down the field to come in for the night. It was winter and the steep field was wet and muddy underfoot, tricky to negotiate even when you're not being pulled in separate directions by ponies both hoping to win the race back to the stable for supper! Anyway, Humbug suddenly stopped, slightly uphill from Annie, and without warning, was up on his back legs, waving his front hooves in Annie's face.

Annie was naturally shocked and as she backed away from the risk of a hoof to the head, he followed her, rearing and punching with alarming accuracy! He has continued ever since to occasionally assault Annie in this way. Maybe he's jealous of her relationship with his pal Toby, we don't know, but she's now very careful at bringing-in time!

18
The Horse Fair

*From horses, we may learn not only about the horse itself
but also about animals in general, indeed about ourselves
and about life as a whole.*
George Gaylord Simpson

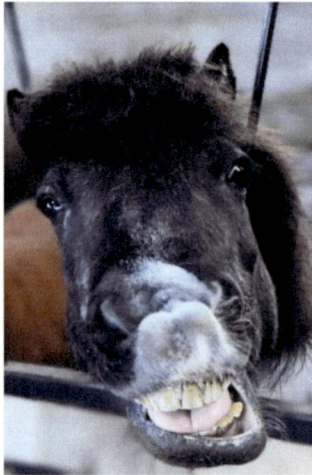

We've learned over the years that buying tack and equipment
for a small, oddly shaped pony is a challenge. Equally
challenging is buying tack and equipment for that pony's even
smaller but perfectly proportioned friend! We heard on the

grapevine that a village less than an hour's drive away holds an auction of horses and equipment every Saturday morning. Our first visit was a real eye-opener. In a dusty carpark behind some industrial units, there were a number of shabby-looking horseboxes, Land Rovers, pick-up trucks and trailers parked haphazardly as their occupants plied their various trades.

Naïvely, we'd turned up in our small, newish car, washed especially for the occasion, and as we locked it and walked away, it was immediately surrounded by grubby, shifty-looking men, all having a look at whether we'd left anything on show in the backseat. We'd worn clean jodhpurs, gilets and smart boots, and stood out like sore thumbs against grimy, sweaty men in filthy, stained vests and jeans!

Young, shifty-looking lads offered what were possibly Jack Russell puppies for £20 each; all far too young to be away from their mum and who looked worm-ridden and poorly. Scrawny hens were £1 each and offered on a very much a 'pick your own' basis from a large, poo-splattered cage in the back of a pick-up truck, presumably ex-battery hens judging by the way they had only a few stubby feathers and many had the ends of their beaks cut off.

A few poorly looking ducks quacked pathetically from a worn wicker basket on the front seat of a Land Rover, while filthy, muck-covered duck eggs were offered for sale by the half-dozen from a basket on the other seat. As we walked on, thinking with dismay that this was nothing like the image we had in our heads, we heard horses' hooves clattering on the concrete. We rounded the corner and were immediately thrust into a full-blown gypsy horse fair.

Skinny teenage lads were trotting their ponies fast and hard on the concrete carpark in front of one of the corrugated metal warehouse units; no saddle, no bridle to speak of, just a piece of rope making a rough, tight noseband as the pony, clearly distressed, went faster and faster, ears back, nostrils flaring, back feet catching the front as the boys showed off their mounts to what they considered the best advantage in order to get a good price.

After a few minutes, the rider jumped athletically to the ground, loud words were exchanged with another boy in what looked to the bystanders as a heated argument, and then suddenly, each spat noisily into his hand and a handshake sealed the deal. I have no idea how much the pony had been sold for as the heavily accented exchange was spoken in words so fast that I couldn't catch them.

The purchaser was clearly not too thrilled with his new mount though, as less than an hour later, we saw him riding the same pony in a similar fashion as yet another bare-chested, swarthy gypsy watched and, presumably, purchased it for an again unknown amount!

There was a long, single-story brick-built building from where we could hear an auctioneer attempting to get the highest possible price for something and we ventured inside for a look. A crowd of elderly men in grubby, sweat-stained shirts blocked our view of the sales ring, so we climbed up the wooden seating area which surrounded the fenced-off sales ring, enabling us to look down on the proceedings.

In the circular pen, its floor sprinkled with sawdust was a poor, emaciated young piebald mare and her equally undernourished dark brown foal, of maybe a month old. The mare was naturally trying to protect her baby, which had a bewildered look on its face, and as she struck out with a hind leg at a man prodding her with a stick, she was delivered a hefty smack across the head which made her teeth rattle. I was horrified and looked at Katie and Annie sitting beside me.

Katie had tears in her eyes as she pleaded with me to buy the pair so we could give them a good home and some decent food. Before she had time to persuade me (and it wouldn't have taken much), a shout went up, the hammer went down, and a deal had been done. I dread to think what became of the mare and her baby, but I can only hope someone else took pity on them and gave them a better life than they'd had so far.

A few more horses went through the ring, some looking like they'd come to the end of their useful working lives, some who looked like typical riding school ponies, and some who looked like they'd come straight off the racetrack! The differences and contrasts between the various horses were amazing, but the one overriding question in my mind was 'why?'. Why are apparently nice, useful horses subjected to such an ordeal when an advert on the internet, or in the local paper would potentially ensure a brighter future?

Maybe owners needed a very quick sale because of a change in circumstances, or maybe they don't want their mount scrutinising too much before money is exchanged for fear of a prospective owner finding that particular fault which will 'unseal' a deal, or maybe, and I really hope this is not the case, a quick sale to the meat man is less costly for the owner than having an old, poorly horse put down humanely by a vet.

I knew I had to get Katie and Annie out of there before they persuaded me to part with cash I couldn't really afford, so we climbed back down the wooden seats and out into another part of the building where we found yet more poor, broken-down horses in pens awaiting their fate. Some owners were trying to arrange their own sales rather than have their horses go through the sales ring and we saw pitiful amounts of money being exchanged for horses that had sad, resigned looks about them.

Finally, we made our way outside and tried to forget the awful sights we'd seen in the holding pens and the ring. We discovered soon after that if we'd arrived later on in the day, the horse auction would have been over and the auctioneer would be enjoying a brisk trade in second-hand tack and equipment. We hung around and visited the questionable on-site café while we waited for the tack auction to start.

The café was an experience in itself; a dull rectangular room with Formica tables and green plastic patio chairs in two rows down each side, a serving hatch at the bottom with what were surely retired school dinner ladies relieving customers of their cash before handing out the food. Each wore a grimy, stained overall and each had a cigarette hanging out of the corner of her mouth, threatening to drop ash into the steaming pots of soup, gravy and custard, all of which were being stirred alternately by the same ladle.

Home-done, poorly spelled tattoos adorned each muscular arm and on each fat finger of their shovel-like hands, diamond and ruby rings twinkled. These sirens of the serving hatch offered a choice of tea or coffee, soup in a mug, bacon or sausage sandwich, and masses of chips; these could be served on a polystyrene tray either with thick gravy slopped over them, or with sauce:

"Reddabraan?"

I was baffled. "…Excuse me?"

It took a few attempts, but eventually, she enunciated carefully, while rolling her eyes sarcastically at the gathering queue. "Red…or…brown…sauce?"

Oh, of course! I couldn't help myself and asked what flavour soup was on offer. I was told it was 'meyt'! And there were 'Deserts' written on a chalkboard at the side of the hatch—'appel' pie and cake, both served with custard. Having observed the stirring of the custard with the gravy-soaked ladle, we opted for neither but amused ourselves by watching an old gypsy man struggling to eat a bacon sandwich while his teeth sat on the table at his side, having been unceremoniously removed moments before.

At the same time, he was grappling with a mangy dog on a string who was grovelling for leftovers, while also trying to contain what I hoped was a ferret wriggling around in his trouser pocket!

By the time we went back into the auction, cheered up by chips and 'people-watching', the sale of tack was well underway—bridles, bits, stirrups, saddles, including a tiny Western-style saddle that would have fitted Toby (I saw Annie's eyes light up and quickly led her away!), and boots for both horse and rider. We bought a few items including a brand-new rug for Spirit, which was less than half the price I would have paid at a 'proper shop', and then we spotted what we'd hoped for—a driving harness that'd fit Toby, but that would extend enough to fit Humbug too.

Some items we won, some we lost to higher bidders, but the fast and furious exchanges were exhilarating to be a part of and we came home with goodies for all of our horses, some for ourselves, and with a determination to ensure that any horse or pony that crosses our threshold never ends up in a place like that.

19
Escapes

He knows when you're happy, he knows when you're
comfortable, he knows when you're confident. And he
always knows when you have carrots!
Unknown (but possibly Humbug!)

Thankfully, Humbug and Toby had decided that they were
best friends right from day one. I say 'thankfully' as they only
had one stable and it could never have been described as
roomy! If they'd decided they hated each other, we would

have had some serious problems on our hands. What we didn't expect, however, was just how comfortable they seemed in each other's company.

If we managed to sneak around to the stable early in the morning, we'd occasionally find the ponies still sleeping; sometimes they'd be curled up together, legs tangled, noses together, both snoring blissfully! On realising they'd been observed, they'd jump up, fart loudly, and then bite each other, pretending they never liked each other in the first place, but we weren't fooled!

In the early years, we were pleasantly surprised at how close the boys were; the fact that they shared a stable led us to assume that once out in the field they'd appreciate a bit of space from each other. However, even when they had other friends to play with, they chose to stay together, mooching around the field together, escaping together, snoozing together, and playing together. We literally never saw one without the other being just a few paces behind. Then one day, Toby was nowhere to be seen.

It was late autumn and the light was fading fast. Humbug refused to come when we called but whinnied loudly while trotting back and forth alongside the wall at the top of the field. My heart sank; Toby was clearly missing and Humbug was stressing near the top of the field, near the gate which led out onto the road. Terrible images ran through my head. Toby is the size of a large dog and in the rapidly fading light, it would be easy for a driver to not realise he was on the road until it was too late.

Annie and I trekked up to where Humbug was creating havoc, shouting and squealing, shaking his mane, and pawing at the ground. We were relieved to see Toby's little ginger face peering through the sheep-wire fence beside the dry-stone wall. Somehow he'd managed to squeeze under a section which separated the main field from a small area used purely for the dumping of tons of cow poo from the barn. This would later be used as fertiliser for the fields, spread from a specially designed (and pretty revolting!) 'muck-spreader' but at that moment, it was quietly rotting down, steaming slightly, and Toby was up to his armpits in it! Humbug was apparently furious that he was just a fraction of a hair's breadth too big to follow and equally furious that Toby was up to naughtiness without him! Sheep-wire is basically 4" squares of fresh air held together with galvanised wire and is widely used by farmers for the purpose of keeping livestock where they want it, but Humbug clearly hadn't read the instruction booklet and could often be seen testing its strength in order to work out the best escape strategy.

He would lean his whole bodyweight against the lengths of wire and if one of the 6" round wooden posts started to 'give', he'd lean harder and harder until the post broke, loosening the once-taut wire which allowed him to push his way under. He'd been observed perfecting this method by the farmer (who'd threatened to shoot him if he continued!) on a number of occasions and then he'd look on in dismay as the posts were either knocked in further or replaced, thereby thwarting his escape plans.

Toby, as far as I know, has never tried this method, but on this occasion must've spotted enough of a gap between the bottom of the fence and the undulating ground beneath it, and done a little limbo dancing to get to the other side!

We had a number of issues to deal with at this point:

(1) How to get Toby back through/under/over the fence,

(2) How to do (1) without getting ourselves covered in poo,

(3) How to do (1) and (2) while keeping Humbug on the correct side of the fence.

Annie, being younger, slimmer, lighter, and a good 30 years more agile than me was designated the short straw and she clambered over the flimsy yet strong wire fencing. I chose while she was straddled, one leg on each side of the wire, to ask, "This fence isn't electrified, is it?"

Annie leapt from the fence and landed a good 10 feet away, startling Toby, who jumped from the sticky poo with a loud squelch! Trying hard to suppress giggles at Annie's reaction, I tried to prise the bottom of the fence from the ground in order to make a big enough gap for Toby to scramble back through. However, Toby clearly thought he'd grown since his arrival on that side of the fence and refused to believe he could fit back under.

Humbug decided to help and pawed angrily at the ground under the fence. Toby backed even further away in alarm. It was almost completely dark when, with Humbug held at arm's length, I held up the fence and pulled hard on Toby's leadrope while Annie gave him a hefty shove from behind. It was a squeeze, but he wriggled through and as we bent the wire back in place, put some flat rocks from the nearby wall on the ground to cover up the gap between the grass and the fence, we congratulated ourselves on a good job well done.

We were convinced that not even the wriggly little stoats who lived in the fields would be able to squeeze past our handiwork.

Guess where both Toby and Humbug were the next day at bringing-in time?

20

Love Is in the Air

The wind whispers in my ear, a secret that I hold so dear. It talks of horses, hills, and trees, of riding in the summer breeze.

Margaret Cagle

As we've already learned, Humbug's number-one love interest has always been Katie. Inappropriately so! As she got older and enjoyed a more independent life of her own, there have naturally been periods where she's stayed away from home, holidays and the like. I still dread these times as Humbug physically and mentally pines for her. He loses weight (although this is not necessarily a bad thing!), his coat becomes dull, and he shows very little interest in anything. Even his usual enthusiasm for food wanes; a sure sign that he's not himself.

When I walk into the stable or the field, he'll look past me as if looking to see if Katie's not far behind, and I've even known him to frisk me as if I'm hiding her in my pockets! When she returns from whichever excursion she has been enjoying, usually suntanned and wearing sandals (not a good idea when Humbug's around!), she has learned to always make a huge fuss of Humbug before she acknowledges any of our other horses; not that she has much choice in this because as soon as he sees her, he's all over her like a rash!

He'll talk to her in his grunty 'hmmphs' as he admonishes her for the abandonment and no doubt tells her how much he has missed her. He'll nip at her legs in his joy and will check all her pockets, sure there are treats and presents hidden in them. Only when Humbug is satisfied that he's made his feelings clear about Katie having left him, and received what he considers a suitable amount of fuss and attention, will he allow the other horses, who've all been waiting patiently, to come forward for their fussing too!

I've always assumed that Humbug was happy to save all his good lovin' for Katie…until the day Ginny arrived! Ginny was also a Shetland pony, the same size and build as Humbug, very pretty, brown and white with a luxurious blonde mane and tail. Ginny had lived for a number of years on a farm not too far away, but her owner, Jen, had driven past our place and had seen Humbug and Toby in the large paddock we'd made for them in the field.

She'd been looking for a new home for Ginny with friends of a similar size as she was being bullied by the bigger horses at her current place, so Jen came along and arranged the move. On the big day, Jen and Ginny walked the short distance along the quiet country roads. Humbug saw her walking up the road and his eyes lit up! He watched her turn off the road and onto our track; he couldn't believe his luck! He let out a loud masculine whinny and she answered with an equally loud but slightly more feminine reply!

Humbug cantered across the field for a closer look and as he and Ginny nuzzled each other through the fence, their love was born. As Jen and Ginny walked down the track, Humbug walked alongside gazing lovingly through the fence the whole way. In parts, the field is higher than the track and at these sections, Humbug raced ahead and waited for Ginny to catch up so that they could continue to walk side by side. Once Jen and Ginny had reached the bottom of the track, Humbug was unable to follow further as he'd reached the very bottom corner of the field.

He pressed his face against the fencing and watched forlornly as Ginny walked away and into the yard. He whinnied pitifully and Ginny's answering whinny seemed just as forlorn. Jen settled Ginny into the stable while she unloaded the car that her son had driven which contained Ginny's few belongings: feed buckets, haynets, headcollars, and, of course, treats. Finally, it was decided that Ginny could join Humbug and Toby in the field for the rest of the day.

They set off back down the way they'd come, only to see Humbug still squashed in the bottom corner of the field with his face pressed hopefully against the fence. He accompanied them the short distance to the gate; Humbug strutting his manly stuff on one side of the fence, Ginny mincing delicately on the other—a perfect match! It was a struggle to get Ginny through the gate as both Humbug and Toby wanted to introduce themselves.

However, once she was in, the three ran around together, tossing their manes, bucking and squealing, and whisking their tails! After a few circuits, they'd slow down and eat a nibble of grass before some unseen signal sent them off again; their twelve short legs a blur as they ran up and down the steep hill, chasing each other and playfully nipping each other's necks. It would have been easy for things to have been spoiled by a lot of jealousy between Humbug and Toby; two male horses and just one female would usually spell disaster as each boy tries to outdo the other in the 'I'm the man' stakes, but there was none of it with these little guys and everyone got on well. We humans watched the antics of the ponies for a while as Jen explained that Ginny was notorious for escaping from paddocks. We laughed and explained that the union between her and Humbug couldn't be more perfect!

Jen assured us that Ginny had only ever escaped if she'd been left alone for any length of time, or if there was more tasty grass on the other side of a fence. We looked back at the ponies who were by now grazing peacefully together and we discussed the 'butter wouldn't melt' theory.

Later the same afternoon, I walked down the track, only to find our electric fencing from which we'd made the ponies' paddock trailing all the way across the field, the very expensive solar-controlled battery pack stamped on and damaged beyond repair, broken fencing posts strewn haphazardly around…and three small fat ponies looking very innocent and quite surprised at the carnage. I was furious and dreaded telling Katie who'd shared the cost of the fencing kit with me as I knew she'd struggle to afford to replace it, as would I.

As I walked around the field collecting what was left of our fencing and picking up the broken posts, I discussed with the ponies that their behaviour had been less than exemplary. They all listened carefully as they checked my pockets for carrots, but each remained tight-lipped about which of them had been the instigator of the annihilation.

The love between Humbug and Ginny remained strong, which although sweet, was sometimes a nuisance. In the early days, if Jen hadn't yet brought Ginny in by the time we were ready to bring the boys in for the night, we'd bring Ginny too, in order to ensure she wasn't left out in the field on her own. It made a sweet picture, the three of them walking politely side by side (by side!) from the field to the yard, but that's when the fun began!

Ginny's stable was in the main block in the yard, and the boys at this point lived around the back in a stable which overlooked the school. Separating them once we reached the yard had its problems as neither of them wanted to leave the other. Toby wasn't quite so troublesome, he was happy to go off and eat his supper, but as we put Ginny into her stable and tried to lead Humbug away, they'd gaze sadly at each other and shout pitifully as each lost sight of the other!

If we tried putting Humbug in the stable first and leading Ginny away, Humbug would kick the walls and the door as Ginny left, so from a preservation point of view, it was best if we put Ginny to bed first!

One of the reasons Humbug and Toby were in a stable away from the main yard was Humbug's health. He'd been diagnosed with COPD (Chronic Obstructive Pulmonary Disease) a couple of years earlier and the vet had recommended a dust-free environment and plenty of fresh air. Not an easy thing to achieve on an old working farm with ancient dusty buildings! We'd started to steam Humbug's hay every day in order to cut down on the dust and spores in it, and they both loved it!

Hay Steamers can be purchased from a number of horsey outlets, but we found they are terribly expensive. Time for a bit of inventive thinking. We bought a large plastic storage box, which had a tightly fitting lid, for around £5, then went to the local DIY place and bought a wallpaper steamer and some rubber hosing. An hour later, we had our own purpose-built steamer for much less than half the price of a 'proper' one! There's something comforting about being in a cold stable on a rainy winter's night with the warmth and smell of steamy hay filling the place! A number of other horse owners have commented that it smells like Shredded Wheat; there's some logic in that I suppose! We also wanted Humbug to have access to fresh air but without the need for him to be out for long periods of time (as already mentioned, he guzzles grass and isn't great at keeping on a muzzle), so we persuaded the farmer to let us use an old, large stable around the back of the main yard. It was actually two stables separated down the middle by a gated partition which we tied back so they'd got the whole thing to play around in.

We used one half for their bed, which at the time was shredded cardboard, so almost completely dust-free, and the other half, the half with the door, we used as their 'daytime quarters' where they had their haynets, water buckets, toys, turnips, and whatever else we felt they'd fiddle around with for entertainment. We even managed to find an old wrought iron garden gate which we talked the farmer into fitting for us rather than a standard door!

It admittedly looked a bit unconventional but it meant both ponies could see out, there was plenty of airflow, they could chat to anyone passing by, and they could watch as their pals were exercised in the outdoor school. I'm sure they've become experts on the various dressage moves over the years as they've watched and listened to a number of riding instructors giving lessons.

The gate didn't provide much protection from the harsh winter weather though and we were worried that the boys would be cold. Thankfully, they were sensible enough to shelter in the back 'bedroom' part in the worst of the weather, but on pleasant days, they'd often be seen snoozing happily and enjoying the warmth of a handy puddle of sun.

21
Of Mice and Mousers

Where in this wide world can man find nobility without
pride, friendship without envy, or beauty without vanity?
Here where grace is laced with muscle and strength by
gentleness confined.
Ronald Duncan

One of the disadvantages of keeping horses and their
equipment on an old working farm was that, occasionally, a
furry family of rodents would take up residence in our rug
store. Worse, they'd take up residence in our rugs! Once or
twice over the years, we realised as we moved a rug from the

rack they were hung on that there'd been the patter of many, many tiny feet and that they were still pattering inside the soft cosy filling of our rugs!

Apart from the damage they caused as they chewed their way in, pulled the stuffing out and made nests, they seemed to produce a ridiculous amount of smelly wee and poo, the aroma of which clung to our rugs and subsequently our horses! We took to encouraging the two ginger farm cats, Max and Paddy, to prowl around the stable, lured inside by a saucer of tasty cat food.

Unfortunately, the cats, being quite elderly at this point, willingly enjoyed the delicious meaty chunks but then didn't see any reason why they would want to expend unnecessary energy in chasing scrawny bite-size mice when saucers of meat were handed out for free! As the cats curled up for a post-lunch snooze on our sunny stone window ledge, we threw up our hands in dismay as we spotted a cheeky mouse brazenly nibbling his way into the lining of an expensive new rug!

We wondered for a while about introducing a couple of cats from an organisation we'd heard of, which rescues feral cats from factories and the like, and releases them onto farms having first undertaken 'the snip' to prevent them from producing more and more feral cats. As we were mulling this idea over, a solution presented itself in our very own garden…or so we thought.

At the time, Katie, Annie, and I lived in a very urban area close to the town centre and the roads over the years had become busier and busier. There was a large hospital less than half a mile away and sirens from ambulances could be heard at all hours of the day and night. In September 2013, we were devastated when one of our own much-loved cats, a big lovable ginger tom called Jasper, was run over and killed right outside our house. He was one of two kittens we'd adopted from the farm many years before and we'd known them from being just a few days old.

We still had his sister, who through her own choice was very much a house cat, but I declared that we'd have no more cats while we lived there as I simply couldn't face the same happening again. One sunny day the following August, I was doodling about in the garden, pulling up weeds (or were they plants? I never know the difference) when I spotted an unfamiliar skinny black cat watching me with wary green eyes from under a section of our laurel hedge.

Almost immediately, she was gone, vanishing apparently into thin air. I lifted the lower branches carefully but she was nowhere to be seen. I'd almost forgotten about her when a few days later, I spotted her once more in the same place. Again, she was watching me with unblinking beautiful bright green eyes, and this time, she maintained eye contact for a couple of seconds before turning tail and disappearing. I caught a momentary glimpse of her running across the road and disappearing down a neighbour's drive, so assuming she belonged to the neighbour, I thought no more about her.

A couple of weeks passed, and I'd all but forgotten the cat when I looked out of my front window and saw not only the now very skinny black cat but also two tiny black kittens! The kittens must have been no more than 3 weeks old and were struggling to stay upright on unsteady legs as their mum licked their fur to keep them looking smart and tidy as they clambered over each other right there in my garden, under my hedge!

I already knew how wary the mum was and managed to resist the temptation to rush out and try to cuddle both her and the babies, knowing that if I startled her, I'd never see them again. I started to wonder where they'd come from. I now knew she didn't belong to the neighbour whose drive she'd run down a couple of weeks previous as I'd received a blank look when I'd asked him how long he'd had a cat! And anyway, no responsible owner would allow such tiny kittens out. It was starting to become clear that they were strays.

Had some uncaring owner dumped her when they realised she was pregnant; or worse, dumped her and the kittens as soon as they were born? I calculated that the kittens would have been newly born when she first appeared in my garden. Was she crying out for help? Food? Shelter? Warmth?

During my musing, a passing car caught my attention and I realised the cat had scarpered again, this time taking her kittens with her—one in her mouth, paws dangling as it was carried along by the scruff of its neck, but the other one was tottering on short legs, tail in the air acting as a rudder as it attempted to cross the road after its mum. My head nearly exploded! I couldn't bear to think of what would happen to these babies if they continued to play Chicken with the busy local traffic.

Quickly, I found a sturdy box, lined it with an old pillow wrapped in a decorating sheet, found an old saucer for food and a small dish for water, and placed them in the sheltered clearing under the hedge where I'd seen the little family. I filled the dishes, one with the expensive dry cat food which our cats had always thrived upon, and the other with clean water, and I sat by the window and waited. And waited! I was terrified at the prospect of the momma cat, let alone the tiny kittens, crossing the road.

However, I naïvely thought that as I'd provided a box to sleep in and a dish of food for mum they'd gratefully live happily in my garden and forget all about their risky traffic-dodging adventures. I anxiously watched from the window as darkness fell and cursed as each car whizzed up and down the road. Eventually, it was night time and it became as dark as it gets in an urban area. It was windy and raining for most of the evening, and although during the course of my cat-watch the food dish had been visited by a hedgehog and a scraggy urban fox, there'd been no sign of the cat family, so after replenishing the food, I went off to bed trying not to worry. I knew Katie and Annie would be as concerned as I was but they were on holiday with their grandparents for the week. I half hoped they'd return home to find me sitting with purring kittens on my lap and the mom curled in front of our log-burning fire warming herself contentedly…

3 days later, Katie and Annie were due back from their holiday and I was eagerly anticipating their stories of lazing by a pool, working on their tans. I heard a car stop and looked out of the window expecting to see them getting out of their grandparents' car. What I actually saw was a car that had braked suddenly, narrowly missed squashing the mother, who was carrying one baby while the other cowered at the roadside in fear!

My heart was in my mouth as I went into the garden, having first grabbed the bag of cat biscuits and a packet of cooked chicken from the fridge. I sat in my front garden, willing the cat to appear as I rattled the bag of cat food and pulled it open. Success! As if from nowhere, the mother's green eyes watched greedily from under the hedge as I poured cat biscuits into the saucer. I sat back and watched as she watched me. I moved a little further back but her eyes never left mine. I retreated further, to the point of sitting on my doorstep, but still, she simply stared.

Ok, you win, I thought as I went into the house and quietly closed the door. I cautiously peered out of the window and was equally relieved and saddened to see the cat gobbling down the biscuits like her life depended on it. She kept a wary eye on me, no doubt ready to bolt if I came back outside, but after she'd polished off the whole dish of food and licked her whiskers clean, she looked pointedly at the packet of chicken that I'd neglected to take back into the house with me.

She retreated under the hedge where she stretched out on her side so her babies could feed and I cautiously crept outside. I reached out slowly for the packet of chicken and pulled out a slice. Momma watched me with those amazing eyes and as I pulled a small piece apart, I tossed it towards the little family. Momma, as quick as a flash, stretched out a paw, claws extended to the tasty morsel, pulling it towards her mouth to gulp it down gratefully.

Another piece went the same way and gradually, over the next half hour, her confidence grew along with her belly! The kittens, fed and happy, played for a while before settling down for a snooze under the branches of the laurel as their mum crept slightly closer, tempted by the chicken that had been intended for lunchtime sandwiches for the following week! After an hour of sitting uncomfortably, I'd persuaded the cat to come close enough to take a piece of chicken out of my fingers!

I was delighted that she was starting to trust me and I spoke gently and calmly to her, telling her how brave she was and how beautiful her babies were. She responded with a low threatening growl and snatched at another morsel of chicken; small talk was clearly not high on her list of priorities!

Suddenly, Katie and Annie were home from their holiday in the sun and as they waved at their grandparents as they drove away, they gave me a very odd look. Apparently, sitting alone in the middle of your front garden, clutching a half-empty packet of chicken is not considered normal behaviour!

"But look, there's a cat and some kittens…" I began, looking at the empty space which only moments before had been occupied by two fast asleep, contented kittens and their relaxed, newly nourished mum! I kept glancing behind me as I followed the girls into the house but the little family had disappeared, again. I wondered as the girls chattered about their holiday, the pool, the beach, and the cocktails, whether the cat and her babies would return and vowed to fill the saucer with biscuits and chicken before bedtime.

Much later, as darkness began to fall, I ventured outside to see three sets of green eyes staring at me from beneath the lower branches of the hedge! I emptied the saucer of dust and leaves and refilled it with more cat biscuits and scraps of the remaining chicken. The eyes stayed where they were, unblinking, as I retreated back into the house. Ruefully, I remembered my fantasy of sitting with purring kittens on my lap. Clearly, it would take a miracle for these nervous, feral creatures to become the cosy lap cats that we were accustomed to.

I looked out of the window, beckoning to Katie and Annie to come and see the cat and her kittens. The girls stood with me at the window as we all peered into the twilight at...nothing. No cat, no kittens, just a saucer filled with biscuits sitting forlornly next to a dish of now dusty water.

It was another three days before Katie and Annie saw any sign of the cat and her babies, and I'm sure they were ready to have me committed! I'd spent a fortune on packets of roast chicken and extra cat food and was constantly peering anxiously into the garden and cringing whenever a car sped up the road. Then, one sunny day, as they arrived home from somewhere in Katie's car, they spotted both kittens fast asleep, curled up together in a pot of geraniums!

They got out of the car quietly and crept as close as they dared. They were as charmed by them as I'd been and quickly joined me in my new habit of sitting in the garden trying to make friends with the mum as she snatched bits of chicken from our fingers. Gradually, they started spending more and more time on our side of the street and I started to relax a little regarding the traffic. But then, one day, I spotted all three of them dodging cars and lorries on the main road that ran along the bottom of our street.

I watched, terrified, as a car narrowly missed the smaller of the two babies as Momma and the larger baby ran onto the pavement. I was in my car, ready to make the turn onto our street, and a car behind me hooted its impatience as I held my breath and watched immobile as Momma went back across the road to collect her kitten and ran yet again through oncoming traffic to the other side. Something needed to be done to capture the family and take them somewhere safe, but how?

I contacted a well-known cat charity and was told to continue gaining the trust of the mother, in the hopes that the kittens would follow suit and be brave enough to approach us for tiny morsels of food. I'd seen them eating from the saucer in the garden, so had started putting out special kitten food for them, which they seemed to relish. The plan then was for the charity to provide a large humane trap which we would start putting their food inside in order to capture all three together.

Over time, the kittens were becoming quite brave and I watched from the window one day as Annie, sitting in the garden, trailed a thin stick along the ground with both kittens chasing it, fascinated! They scurried back and forth in a hunting frenzy as they almost, but not quite caught the stick. Slowly as Annie held out a hand, they sniffed at her and then cautiously climbed onto her lap. They quickly scrambled back down again but contact had been made and accepted.

Suddenly, I realised I potentially had my very own solution to the mouse problem at the farm! I rang my friend, Fran, and floated the idea with her. Although she wasn't as enthusiastic as I'd hoped, she agreed to maybe have the momma and one kitten as long as they were 'fixed' so they couldn't produce more. Ok, I'd cross that bridge when I came to it but felt confident that at least two of them had found a great home.

My son, Sam, who by this time had moved out and was renting his own place, which he shared with a couple of mates, had on a few occasions wondered about getting a cat as he'd missed ours since moving out. That was great then; all three could be rehomed as soon as we could catch them.

Typically, things didn't go according to plan…

As we managed to gain the trust of the kittens, they were easily caught and lived for what I thought would be a couple of days in a large dog cage in our kitchen. They were painfully thin, which had been disguised well by their fluffy coats. However, by the time they'd been de-flead, de-wormed, and had regular feeds, they started to put on weight and their fluff gradually became sleek fur. They would have been around 9 or 10 weeks old by this point and were perfectly able to be away from their mother.

They still slept curled up together and although, at first, we thought they were identical, we noticed that the smaller of the two had a few white hairs under her chin. The other, slightly fatter one, was less skittish and became brave enough to approach us when we let them out of the cage to change the litter tray and refill the food and water dishes. She would creep up on us and cautiously climb using her tiny needle-sharp claws onto our laps if we sat on the floor. As soon as we moved, however, she'd leap down again, only to restart the whole process as soon as she'd regained her courage!

She was desperate to be friends and it was a proud moment when we first heard her purr loudly while being stroked on a handy lap! Following the wormer and the good food, I felt they'd better go to their respective homes before I became too attached. We'd not seen the mum since the day we caught the kittens and, although food was still disappearing from the dish in the garden, I couldn't be positive it was being eaten by her.

I saw Fran one night when I was bringing the horses in and asked when I could bring her tiny new mouser. Her eyes shifted away from mine. "Oh yes, about that…" she started.

It turned out she'd changed her mind and decided that with the elderly farm cats she already had, it would be unfair to introduce a young kitten to the mix. Not to worry, I'd just persuade Sam he wanted both kittens. I rang him that night.

"Actually, Mum, we've heard today that we've got to move out as the landlord is selling the house, so I won't be able to have one. And anyway, we barely remember to feed ourselves, so I don't fancy a kitten's chances much. Unless it's happy to live on beer…" Aaagghhh!

I rang the lady at the cat charity with whom I'd spoken previously and explained my predicament. I also added that having recently sold my house, I was due to move within the next couple of months and really didn't want to be taking semi-feral, semi-grown kittens with me. The kindly charity worker agreed that they'd provide funding for neutering and, if necessary, would also provide food and litter if I'd keep them just until they could find a foster home for them.

She advised me to socialise them as much as possible to make them more adoptable and said that they'd ring me when they'd found them a suitable foster parent. I felt horribly guilty as I played with the kittens later that day as I felt the pair were starting to really trust us. The chubbier one was happy to be cuddled and stroked, and although the other smaller one hadn't yet been brave enough to do the same, progress was definitely being made.

Although I'd turned down the offer of food and litter, I was grateful that the neutering operation would be taken care of, as I felt this would make them more attractive to prospective new owners. A couple of weeks later, I'd heard nothing further about rehoming them and I rang the charity. I was told they were struggling to find a foster home as apparently black kittens are not as attractive as the 'pretty' ones (really!) and that, unfortunately, they were overrun with kittens at the moment.

Though not to worry as they'd be back to me as soon as possible with details of when I could hand them over. Again, guilt ate away at me and I tried to harden my heart to these cute little fluffy bundles of fun, which I'd seen grow from being tiny babies... No, stop! I really didn't want to be moving house with yet more animals; we already had two dogs, six chickens, our own cat, a house rabbit who thought he was a dog, a goldfish (who, for reasons I now can't remember was called Herpes!), 40+ pond fish, and two turtles to pack up and move.

No, they had to be rehomed... Didn't they? I'd resolutely avoided naming the kittens with the theory that as I would never need to call them to me, they didn't need names, but we were starting to refer to them as The Fat One and The Naughty One. Hardly fair! One of Annie's favourite programmes on TV when she was a toddler had a character called 'Ojo'. Suddenly, The Fat One became Ojo and quite naturally, The Naughty One became Mojo. Well, they could go to their new home already knowing their names, I reasoned.

Suddenly, the day of the big operation arrived and we bundled them both unceremoniously into a travelling box and drove to the vet. We warned the receptionist that the kittens were still semi-feral and she made a note on her computer. 5 minutes later, 'Kittens Gilbert' were called into the surgery. The vet was a large, loud, jolly-hockey-sticks kind of lady and as she undid the cage front of the box, I reminded her that the kits were feral.

"Oh, I love it when mummies call their naughty kitties feral," she hooted as she stuck her arm into the box. Yowls and growls and snarls emitted from the depths and her arm retreated much more quickly than it went in! She had a half-grown, semi-feral kitten attached to her forearm and as she vigorously shook her arm, the kitten along with an array of blood splatters decorated the wall! The kitten (Mojo, aka The Naughty One) clung by her claws to a cork noticeboard, and somewhere at the back of my mind I thought, *I did warn her.*

Mojo suddenly regained her bearings and proceeded to execute an impressive 'Wall of Death' manoeuvre around the surgery, the type of thing more often seen done by motorcyclists in fairgrounds. The vet was still bleeding profusely and she shouted loudly through the closed door into the back for help. I could only imagine what the gathered pet owners out the front thought when they heard her cries. I'd gone in there with a small box containing two cute mewing kittens and suddenly a large, loud lady vet was yelling for help!

A nurse quickly bandaged up the still bleeding vet and with what I thought was a satisfied smirk, not quite hidden, she soon produced a towel and a pair of thick leather gloves. She efficiently caught Mojo under the towel and, armed with the gloves, she stuffed her back into the box with her sister. She avoided making eye contact, although I definitely detected a slight grin playing around her lips as she advised me to pick them up in a couple of hours.

I left the surgery aware that I was the recipient of troubled glances from the other pet owners in the waiting room. I got into the car and realised, as I looked in the rear-view mirror, that I was liberally splattered with vet blood!

Just a few days later, Ojo and Mojo were back to their usual selves and I contacted the charity, yet again, to ask if there'd been any progress on the rehoming. It was during a conversation with the receptionist that the 'light bulb' turned on and the obvious dawned on me…they'd already found my kittens a very nice home, with a dedicated owner who would happily cater to their every whim—me! All this time I'd been fostering the kittens for them, feeding them, socialising them, and even arranging for them to be neutered. I'm surprised I wasn't on the payroll!

A couple of months later, the girls and I moved house; we left our urban life behind and moved with all our belongings, and our ever-expanding family of animals, to a little house on the edge of a rural village between Sheffield and Huddersfield. From our windows, we could see fields full of cows and horses, and just down the road, about 100 yards away, there was a field with a Shetland pony! The cats (all three of them!) settled in like they'd always lived there.

Cat wisdom suggests keeping your family moggy indoors for a few weeks when you move house before letting it venture out into the garden, supervised closely. However, ours all had a mooch around the garden on the first day, sat on top of the chicken house in the sun, rolled around happily in the flower beds, and watched the removal guys unloading the lorry containing all of our belongings, before coming back inside to demand their suppers. It seemed life in the countryside with three cats wasn't going to be that much more complicated than with one!

The following morning, I awoke early and sat in my new living room, surrounded by boxes, with a steaming mug of coffee in my hand. Nestled cautiously but purring contentedly in my lap for the very first time was Mojo! Clearly, she was going to enjoy being a countryside cat and I scratched her behind the ear. I could only rejoice that our new rural life should be relatively free from rodents!

22
Time to Move On

I have seen things so beautiful, that they have brought tears to my eyes; yet none of them can match the gracefulness and beauty of a horse running free.
Author unknown

There were times when, because of Rio's various ailments, Humbug's COPD, and Spirit's advancing years, I wondered if a Yorkshire hill farm was the right home for our horses. We all loved the farm and the people there, particularly the farmer's wife, Glenda, who was a loving, supportive surrogate mum to us all. We'd shared Christmases, Easters, births, deaths, marriages, divorces, friendships, and squabbles, but more and more the idea of a less hilly environment with airier stables was becoming increasingly attractive.

My friend, Fran, who'd lived on the farm for so many years, had by this point moved with her new husband to a farm of their own, so the pull to stay there had, for me at least, lessened slightly. I cautiously broached the subject of finding our horses a new home to Katie and Annie. Katie was surprisingly willing to discuss the subject as she was aware that Rio was struggling more and more with the steep hills. Annie, however, was horrified!

The farm had featured so prominently in my family's upbringing and the memories my children had of growing up there were held dear. Annie couldn't bear the idea of us not going there every day and it seemed that no amount of reasoning with her would change her mind. Several months passed, and I'd pretty much given up on my musings of moving when a friend at work told me about a brand-new equestrian centre that she and some of her friends were moving their horses to.

It sounded amazing—flat, grassy paddocks, well-made post-and-rail fences, sparkly new white painted stables in a light, airy Dutch barn all with automatic water drinkers installed, two outdoor schools, a lunging pen, a full set of jumps, plans for an indoor arena, miles of countryside hacking (with no roads!) direct access onto the Trans Pennine Trail…and only a few miles away from where we now lived. I sneakily went for a quick look during one lunch break without telling Katie or Annie that I was going. I was blown away by how smart the new place looked.

It had been open literally just a couple of weeks and the whole place still shone! Even the muck heap looked clean! A far cry from our shabby, cobwebby, ancient stables back 'home'. I drove back to work deep in thought and just happened to run into the colleague who'd by then moved her horse there. She told me how happy and settled he was, and how her daughter, who was a couple of years younger than Katie, was looking forward to the summer; hacking out with friends and taking part in the shows that the yard manager was promising to arrange.

Wasn't this just what we'd always wanted? Long summer hacks on well-made, level tracks, not having to worry about whether drivers will slow down when we're out hacking and none of the steep hills that made Rio's joints so sore? I took the plunge and rang the yard manager to make an appointment for a proper look around and to discuss prices for DIY livery. She admitted that so far, she only had horses there whose owners paid to have much of the day-to-day care done by staff, so wasn't entirely sure of how much to charge us when we'd be doing everything ourselves.

We haggled very politely for a few minutes, as only the British can, and we finally settled on what we both thought was a fair price for three stables (she was amused that the ponies share!). I was pleasantly surprised to discover that our lot could live there for hardly any more than we were already paying. Interesting! I asked if I could have a couple of days to think things over and to bring Katie and Annie for a look around.

Naturally, she told me that demand was high and if I left it too long, she would have other people wanting to bring their horses…she didn't know when there'd be further vacancies…if we missed this opportunity we could perhaps go on a waiting list but three stables together might not be available again. I tried not to be taken in by the subtle yet high-pressure sales pitch but quickly arranged to take Katie and Annie to have a look around!

That same evening, Katie had ended up having a 'heated discussion' with the new yard manager at our place; some confusion about wanting a bale of hay for the ponies on a Wednesday when the YM wanted hay to be purchased on a Saturday, and the crime of the century—Katie had left the gate of the arena open when she brought Rio out after riding her. Katie had already found herself in the YM's firing line earlier in the week when she'd had to change the 'field poo-picking rota' as Katie was working on the day she'd been allocated. YM took this as a personal affront and told Katie, in front of other owners, how inconvenient her 'messing things around' was. All too stupid for words really, but the stupidity helped to make the decision which, at the back of our minds, we kind of knew was inevitable. I'd told Katie about the stables, the paddocks, the smart wooden fences (Humbug-proof?), the access onto the Trans Pennine Trail, the plans for the indoor school (a luxury we'd until now only ever dreamt of!), and she was keen to check it out for herself.

We all visited on a bright sunny afternoon and another owner greeted us as we got out of the car. She introduced herself and as we chatted, she told us how happy her three 'boys' were since moving a couple of weeks ago. It turned out, that her 'boys' were all impressively well-bred dressage horses working their way up the ranks and are now quite well-known stars! We told her about our mixed bunch and she was enthused about the ponies.

Apparently, she'd always wanted a Shetland (most people do until they meet Humbug!) and she couldn't wait to see them. The yard manager appeared, in pristine white jodhpurs, spotless shirt and waistcoat, and expensive leather boots, and showed us around again, discussed which of the available stables we wanted, where our bedding, tack, harnesses, feed, etc., could be kept. Suddenly, we'd arranged to move the following Monday! We got back into the car to return home and all burst into tears! How could we be doing this?

It seemed ludicrous to think that I was planning to move Spirit from the home she'd known for 16 years! And the logistics of moving 16 years' worth of 'stuff' was starting to dawn on me too.

We had a total of twenty-seven rugs, four sets of tack, plus two sets of driving harnesses, two carts, first aid equipment, lotions and potions, four grooming kits, dozens of haynets, feed buckets, water buckets, bags and bins of feed (and each horse has a different menu!), Thirty-plus bags (each 25 kg) of bedding, a set of show jumping poles, miles of electric fencing and posts, rubber flooring for the stables, a couple of wheelbarrows, mucking-out equipment... The list was going on and on!

After a sleepless night, and a couple of more teary moments at work the following day, I decided to take the next fortnight as a holiday (holiday!) from work and concentrate on getting things arranged.

The first job was to tell the family at the farm that we'd be leaving. Even now, thinking about that conversation can reduce me to tears, and it was with a heavy heart that I explained to Glenda that we had to do what was right for our horses. Rio would have more useful years if we looked after her legs and joints, Spirit too deserved a less hilly pace of life now that she was in her dotage, and Humbug...well to be honest, Humbug would be happy wherever Katie was, but a cleaner, less dusty environment could only be a good thing for him.

We then told the other horse owners, all of whom were completely shocked, as they considered us to be part of the fabric of the place. We'd been there longer than anyone; in fact, Spirit was the first horse on the place since Grandad Jack's Shire horses worked the land many, many years ago! As conversations went on, we realised we weren't the only ones thinking of moving as the YM was upsetting a number of people with her unfriendly manner and unreasonable rules.

The next week or so was very odd; there was definitely a feeling of 'an elephant in the stable' as we tried to go about our usual horsey activities—riding, mucking out, and feeding—while all the time not mentioning that in just a matter of days, we'd be gone.

I rang the company we'd previously hired the horse lorry from, expecting to book it for a couple of days so we could move everything in that. 'No, sorry, we don't have anything available' was the phrase that threw the spanner in my loosely arranged works! Now what? I turned to the internet and started ringing around a long list of horse transport self-drive hire places. Several hours later, I was running out of options.

It turned out we'd chosen to move on the same weekend of a large 3-day agricultural show in the area and everyone who had horses but no wheels had already booked every single lorry for miles around. Panic had already set up camp when finally, a lady told us she'd had back word on a lorry as it was too small for her customer's horses and he'd changed his mind! Thank goodness for men who ride big horses!

The lorry was a good hour and a half's drive away but we could pick it up on Sunday night and take it back Monday night, giving us plenty of time to move everything and everybody…or so we naïvely imagined!

23
A New Home

No, I don't need a knight in shining armour; I'm quite
capable of riding my own horse!
Author unknown

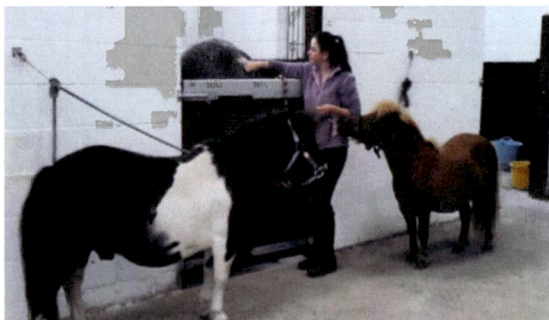

We started bright and early on Monday morning, loading all of our horses' belongings into the lorry. We'd collected it as arranged the night before, leaving my car at the yard to pick up later, and had meticulously planned several journeys carrying all the equipment before the final two journeys: one carrying Humbug and Toby and the last one carrying Spirit and Rio. It all went so well until Spirit refused to load! We'd got a little behind time anyway as we were simply running out of energy. Loading and unloading everything was hard work and we'd not accounted for people at the new place introducing themselves and their horses, and chatting to us every time we pulled into the car park to unload the lorry. Finally, it was time to load the ponies and we'd already noticed that Humbug had spotted the lorry from the field. He'd kept an eye on proceedings throughout the day, watching carefully each time we drove in or out of the yard, but this time, we drove the lorry around to where they were waiting! He was beside himself with excitement and whinnied loudly from the field gate as Katie and Annie walked towards them with headcollars. I admit to again having tears in my eyes as the girls walked them away from their pals in the field for the very last time, but tears soon turned to laughter as Humbug charged purposefully towards the lorry and dragged Katie up the ramp! He'd clearly decided it was high time he enjoyed a road trip and there was no way we were taking it anywhere again without him on board!

The lorry had a camera installed, with the monitor in the cab, so we could watch during the journey to make sure they were ok. We'd already decided it was pointless tying Humbug up to the handily positioned tie-rings as he'd simply untie himself and torment Toby, so we left them both loose; maybe not a great idea for most horses but for these two, it was the only way to do it!

We watched them wander around as we set off driving, and after a couple of minutes, Toby worked out that if he wedged himself in the corner, he could travel without falling as we negotiated the steep hills and sharp turns. Humbug preferred the white-knuckle style of travelling and stood sideways on, just to add to the rollercoaster effect. Half an hour later, they arrived at their new home and we bedded them down in their brand-new, never-been-used-before stable.

We felt really guilty for leaving them so soon after they arrived somewhere unfamiliar but we filled their haynets and assured them we'd be back soon with Spirit and Rio. Little did we know that it'd be another 4 hours before we could persuade Spirit to clamber aboard the lorry!

Spirit had undergone a full health check by the vet during the week as I was concerned that the stress of moving might not be good for her 22-year-old heart. However, the vet declared her fit and well, and in good condition so she was prescribed a mild sedative, to be administered half an hour before we intended to travel. This was supposed to 'take the edge off' any anxieties she felt about loading onto the lorry and make the journey less stressful for her.

However, once sedated and drowsy, she placed one hoof on the ramp of the lorry and completely freaked out! Unfortunately, and in hindsight very naïvely, despite all of our planning and organising, I'd not come up with a 'Plan B' in case anyone didn't want to travel! We tried again and again to persuade her to walk up the ramp; sometimes she got two hooves on, sometimes three, but never four. Each time we were close to her thinking it was ok, she'd suddenly panic and jump off again, dragging me around the yard with her!

I was jumped on, stamped on, pushed over, kicked, squashed, and generally battered by my admittedly temperamental mare, who I've chosen to assume was genuinely scared of going onto what must have looked to her like a biscuit tin on wheels. Mild frustration turned eventually to desperation. The lorry was due back at 7 pm, an hour and a half's drive away, and at 7.30 pm, Spirit was still nowhere near loading!

In an attempt to persuade Spirit that the lorry didn't have monsters lurking in the corners, we loaded Rio, who, it has to be said, was less than impressed at being shut in when all the fun was still happening outside. It had started raining, we were cold and wet, Spirit's sedative had long since worn off, and to make matters worse, we now had a gawping audience of other horse owners, all of whom typically had different advice to dispense!

Finally, a team of ten people was set up. I was sent around the corner so I couldn't watch and Spirit was pushed, pulled, prodded, and bullied onto the lorry by the assembled crew. Not the way I wanted things to go by any means, but once on, she looked out of the little window at us, with an expression on her face that clearly said 'Well, come on then, what are we waiting for?'.

Rio and Spirit actually seemed to enjoy the short journey and watched happily through the windows as the world went by. Half an hour later, Spirit walked calmly off the lorry along with Rio and we showed them to their new accommodation. The owner of the lorry had already left an anxious message on my phone, so I rang to explain that we'd had 'a little trouble' with loading. She was relieved that I'd not wrapped her precious (and expensive!) lorry around a tree somewhere and she informed me that as long as it was cleaned out and back before the following morning, when it was booked out again, then there was no problem. After checking that everyone had arrived unscathed, making a huge fuss of Humbug and Toby to apologise for abandoning them, we left Katie to finish bedding everyone down and Annie and I cleaned out the lorry (nervous horses poo…a lot!) before starting the 90-minute journey to return it.

It was by now turned 10 pm and we were utterly exhausted! Just before midnight, we arrived at the livery yard from where we'd hired the lorry and began the embarrassing task of waking up the owner, who came out in her pink dressing gown and fluffy slippers to carry out the exchange of keys, etc. I'd left my car in her driveway when we'd collected the lorry (several weeks ago, surely!), so after apologising profusely for the lateness, Annie and I set off yet again to drive back to our new yard to collect Katie, who'd stayed to make sure everyone was calm and settled in their new stables.

What a day…and just as we arrived home, we realised we'd not eaten since breakfast! Thank goodness for the local drive-through!

24

More Escapes

For through his mane and tail, the high wind sings. Fanning
the hairs, who wave like feather'd wings
William Shakespeare, Venus and Adonis

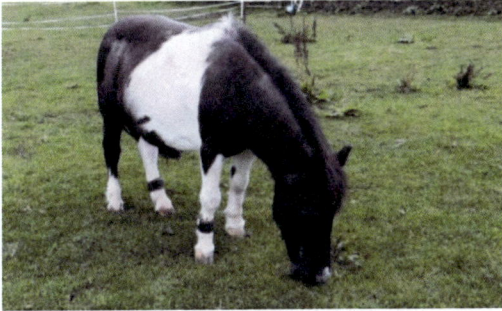

The following morning dawned bright and sunny. Much brighter and sunnier than we all felt, having crawled exhausted into our beds only 4 hours earlier! But it was time to introduce the horses to their stablemates and show them their new paddocks! We could hardly wait and drove to the new yard in excited anticipation!

As we drove down the track, between lush, green paddocks, we became a little concerned, as all of the fields behind the smart wooden post-and-rail fences were divided into paddocks by lengths of electric fencing, the lowest strand of which was at least a metre high. Two small ponies could easily walk straight under. Hell! Had we not mentioned how vertically challenged our Shetlands were? We turned into the car park and as we saw other owners' cars, the nerves suddenly kicked in.

It felt like the first day in a new job when you have to fix a bright smile onto your face and walk into an unfamiliar office, amongst a bunch of people that you don't know, and try your best to make a good impression. As we walked nervously into the barn, cheery shouts of 'Good morning' greeted us. Someone handed us each a mug of coffee and offered a jar of biscuits, and people were bustling around, bantering good-naturedly as they fed, groomed, and tacked up their horses. What a lovely atmosphere!

The lady we'd met on our visit a couple of weeks previously greeted us and admitted guiltily that she'd already fed half a packet of ginger biscuits to the ponies! As we laughed at her admission, Humbug heard Katie's voice and squealed his indignation at not being able to see her. There came a swift tattoo of hoof beats against the wooden door and Katie rushed over to prevent him from destroying it. As she greeted the main man in her life, we pondered the likelihood of having the door adjusted so they could see out.

Spirit and Rio were enjoying looking over their stable doors, taking an interest in their new surroundings and pulling faces at their neighbours. Humbug and Toby could only see the painted walls of their stable and clearly felt that they were missing out. They could hear as horses were led out to the paddocks and their ears flicked back and forth as they tried to work out where they were and where their, as yet unseen, stablemates were going off to.

A moment or two later, a portly gentleman dressed in tweeds strode into the barn with an air of propriety about him. The assembled owners greeted him warmly, and we were informed by our new biscuit-brandishing friend that he owned the whole huge farm that our livery yard sat upon. He greeted us jovially and peered over the door at the 'Little Chaps' as he'd already dubbed them. "How would it be if I replaced this door with one half the height?" He suggested. Perfect!

Within just a couple of days, the ponies had a door perfectly proportioned to their size, meaning they could look out and watch the bustle of a busy livery yard. This also meant, of course, that the staff who worked there, and the owners of the other seventeen horses in the adjoining stables could be persuaded by Humbug that he was a poor, starving pony that needed just one more biscuit in order to survive.

We'd started to worry for the health of the ponies, bearing in mind the amount of sugar they were consuming when each owner fed them 'just one' ginger biscuit every day. However, nature took its course and once Humbug had nipped everyone a few times, their cuteness somehow seemed to wear off and the biscuit jar remained full.

That first day, we still had the issue of the un-Shetland-proof fencing to deal with. We walked the girls out to their allocated paddock and watched as they wandered around finding their bearings with thankfully happy expressions on their faces. They sniffed at their new neighbours, squealed and nipped noses briefly before lowering their heads to graze contentedly, whisking their tails lazily in the sunshine. We resisted the temptation to simply lean on the fence watching, and resigned ourselves to digging out the fence posts and electric fencing from the space we'd been allocated in the large metal storage container.

We set to work creating a pony prison which would contain the two fuzzy monsters. An hour or so later, with hands that were shredded from the sharp wire threads in the fencing tape, we had a paddock with fencing at such a height that we could turn out the boys into it, reasonably confident that they'd still be in it later on. They were delighted to be out in the sun again and sunk to their knees to roll around ecstatically on their backs, waving their hooves in the air, before jumping up, farting loudly, and running around happily, chasing and nipping each other.

We were satisfied that everyone was happy with their new home and walked back to the stables to muck out.

An hour later, full of yet more coffee and biscuits, we had three clean and swept stables, full haynets ready for the evening and we decided to wander up to see how our horses were getting along. As we walked up the track in the warm sunshine, we spotted lots of little brown birds scuttling around in the long grass. We realised they were pheasant chicks, still unable to fly, hence the scuttling! Some of them seemed almost tame and were in serious danger of being stood on as they failed to move out of our way as we made our way between the various paddocks.

We later learned that the farmer raises pheasants for the local gentry to shoot and someone had left open the gate to their pen, hence them being in our fields.

It was as we neared the pony paddock that we noticed Toby grazing…alone! Our hearts sank; they'd been out in the field for less than 2 hours and already the beast was loose! We hoped and prayed he'd not gone through the main gate onto the road, but as we scanned the horizon for a ball of black and white fluff, we spotted him in the paddock with Spirit and Rio. He was grazing happily with his big sisters, who, it has to be said, were unimpressed at him sharing their allocation of grass and were pulling evil faces at him.

We realised that in order to go and find them, he'd crossed three other paddocks with unfamiliar horses in each—one of which, a large, elderly mare called Dash, we now know is always kept in a paddock on her own as she is very aggressive towards other horses. Humbug either ran very, very quickly through her patch or somehow charmed her into letting him through unscathed. Katie shouted his name and he looked up, cheeks bulging with grass, and greeted her with his trademark 'hmmph!'.

He whinnied to her and came trotting towards us, happily ducking under Spirit and Rio's fence, swerved skilfully past Dash, who looked like she was planning to eat him, and briefly visited an excitable grey thoroughbred called Bliss, who was more than happy to run around with him until he remembered his mission was to get to Katie and tell her of his adventures.

After discussing with him the danger he'd potentially put himself in, we posted him back into the paddock with Toby and set about fixing the gap he'd made, while he watched with a carefully uninterested expression on his face. We had no doubts that if we left Spirit and Rio several paddocks away, he'd visit regularly, potentially injuring himself in the fencing, or ending up as a tasty snack for Dash!

We negotiated a paddock swap with my colleague whose horse, William, was in the paddock next to the ponies.

William, we were told, would be more than happy to move as there was more grass in the one that Spirit and Rio had been in further along the track, so thankfully, we didn't cause too much disruption, and with Spirit and Rio next door, Humbug didn't feel the need to escape again…for a while!

25
Settling In

Whoever said the horse was dumb, was dumb.
Will Rodgers

Predictably, Humbug waited until we felt confident he wouldn't escape again before he escaped again! And once he'd become proficient, there was no stopping him. We'd used so much fencing tape, that it looked like he was in a knitted paddock, but still, he'd randomly appear in other horses' paddocks, on the track, in the yard, in the barn. It was becoming clear that he wouldn't be contained by simple electric fencing and we were running out of ideas.

One late summer afternoon, Henry, the farmer, approached us in his usual self-important manner, striding purposefully over to us fully dressed in his trademark tweed, including tie and waistcoat, deerstalker hat perched upon his head, and a muddy gundog at his heels. "How would it be if the Little Chaps had their own field?" He boomed.

He'd witnessed Humbug being Humbug on a couple of occasions, and although he found him very entertaining, was concerned that he'd end up somewhere he shouldn't. He strode off, calling over his shoulder to us, "Come along!"

Katie and I trotted obediently in his wake, up a steep slope that ran at an almost 45-degree angle up a hill behind the small outdoor sand-covered arena where we owners exercised our horses. At the top of the slope was a narrow open gateway and Henry stood, hands on hips, surveying the square field beyond. Sturdy wooden post-and-rail fencing bordered three sides, including the side that overlooked the small outdoor school, and a 5-foot-high dry-stone wall made the fourth.

"I've had horses in here before but their sodding big feet buggered up the grass," he informed us. "I've looked at the Little Chaps' feet and I think they'll be fine in here."

We weren't brave enough to disagree with him but we felt that 'the Little Chaps' and their tiny hooves would make a real mess of the field in wet weather. He strode away again, shouting, "I'll get the boys to put a gate on tomorrow if it doesn't bloody rain, and then it's all yours," leaving us standing gawping after him.

Sure enough, the following day, two builders were measuring, sawing, and hammering, and suddenly, a brand-new wooden gate had been fitted onto shiny new hinges and our 'Little Chaps' had their very own field! Humbug and

Toby were delighted with their new playground and immediately put their heads down to taste the sweet grass. It didn't take long for curiosity to kick in though, and Humbug strolled casually over to the fence so that he could test the boundaries.

We watched him lean his whole bodyweight on the wooden fencing and his face fell as it stayed firm. He wandered nonchalantly over to the wall, but it too wasn't going to give and eventually, he decided to eat some grass while he thought things over. A few days passed and Humbug still hadn't escaped. Success! What he had done in those few days, however, was traumatise every horse and rider who entered the arena below his perimeter fence.

Some owners, including us, had full-time jobs, so had no option but to exercise their horses during the evenings in the floodlit schooling arena. Humbug worked out that his little whiskery face suddenly appearing through the fence in the gloomy darkness had his big pals scared out of their wits! He seemed thoroughly amused by the terror he struck into both horse and rider. The horses bolted to the opposite side of the school, snorting in fear, eyes wide, and nostrils flaring at the furry little monster that was looming above them.

Often riders stayed aboard, but the ones who didn't, returned to the barn with a tell-tale coating of sand on their jodhpurs, coat and hat! Not everyone was amused by Humbug's game of terror and a few asked if they could bring the ponies into the stable before they rode. We made a point of letting everyone know where the ponies' headcollars were kept and we made sure a filled haynet was always hung in the stable for them, just in case!

The first winter at the new yard was a revelation! Previous winters had seen us walking the horses out on cold, windy mornings to slippery, wet, muddy fields, knowing that several hours later, we'd be washing 16 filthy legs in cold water before putting the horses to bed, only for the whole thing to be repeated the next day. Winters on a Yorkshire hillside are long, cold and wet! The new yard, however, had 'winter paddocks' sectioned off for each horse, with nice firm sand underfoot, a wooden post where a haynet could be tied, and an automatic water trough set in each section.

Initially, we worried that they'd hate what we'd dubbed the 'Pony Prison', but by mid-November, we were eating our words as the horses seemed very happy spending the day in their allocated plot! The paddocks were sheltered from the wind as the whole area had been cut from a corner of the hillside, so there were steep cliff sides on three sides, with tall trees on the tops providing yet further protection from the weather.

Initially, it seemed to us to be a very unnatural way for the horses to be kept, and I admit to having voiced my concerns to anyone who'd listen, but Spirit and Rio happily walked to their plots in the mornings, mooched around all day and chatted to their neighbours, while eating tasty, easily accessed hay; a far cry from paddling around up to their knees in mud, searching out the odd blade of grass as they'd previously known. And the indulgence didn't end there. At the bottom end of the stable block was—luxury beyond luxury—a heated shower and an overhead solarium!

Admittedly, it took a few tries to persuade Spirit that she wasn't going to be microwaved, but once she stood under the lights, gently warming her ageing back and neck, she relaxed and started to realise the benefits of winter at the new yard. Humbug, surprisingly, didn't like the solarium at all. The first time we put him in there for a 15-minute session, we lowered the overhead light contraption to its lowest position and switched it on, expecting him to enjoy the experience. Humbug always surprises us.

After just a minute or so, he started to fidget, then shocked us by rearing, bucking, and snorting to make his feelings known. We quickly removed him but soon realised that his objection wasn't to the solarium itself, but the lack of activity while he was in there! 15 minutes with nothing to do, nobody to annoy, and nobody to bite was just a step too far! He sometimes objected to the shower too. Humbug predictably can still come in from the field muddy, even if he's rugged up from his ears to his tail! He's an enthusiastic roller and finds the squishiest mud to indulge in this pastime! We often have to clean mud from the inside of his rugs and often ask ourselves 'How on earth?'. He occasionally had to go to bed muddy at the hill farm home, however, here he could be showered and dried off in the stable block.

The walls of the shower cubicle had tie-rings so the horses, once in there, could be 'cross-tied' to each side, enabling their owners to manoeuvre around them and still be as safe as possible. Humbug managed the first time to rear and hook his feet over the ropes attaching him to the walls, making him appear as if he was hung in some kind of cat's-cradle apparatus.

After untangling him, we decided it best if he's 'hand-held', although this gave him the opportunity to run in circles around whoever was daft enough to try and shower him, thus tangling up himself, the human, the shower, and anything else he could disrupt along the way. He was also likely to stop running at any given moment and drop to his knees to roll around on the wet, dirty floor, making himself filthier and wetter than when he went in there in the first place!

26

Intruder Alert

No one can teach riding so well as a horse.
C. S. Lewis

So, we made it through the first winter happily, with the added bonus of knowing that there were staff on site in case we couldn't get through the ever-threatening snow. Being unable to get to the horses in the thick of winter has always been one of my worries and there had been many mid-winter evenings when the children were little that we'd had to abandon our car and trudge through deep snow for the last couple of miles to the hill farm.

Although this is exciting for children, particularly as we'd take sledges and the excited dog, it can be very stressful for a mum wondering how she's going to get them all home safely again, and I was glad that at the new yard, some of that stress had been alleviated. Often, after settling the horses in for the night, we'd make ourselves a mug of steaming coffee in the kitchen area, and, assuming Humbug didn't help himself to it, we'd drink it while we chatted with the other owners or grooms, munching on the ever-present biscuits and planning the next day's ride or schooling session.

Usually, Katie and I were the last ones there at night and we'd enjoy taking the opportunity to let Humbug indulge his passion for 'escaping'. We'd lock the big barn doors and let him out of his stable! He'd wander happily around the barn, picking up bits of hay from the front of each stable, and enjoy a chat with each horse, before eventually making his way back to his own stable where Toby, who wouldn't have even noticed the open door, would be munching on his haynet!

Suddenly, we'd made it through the worst of the winter and it was spring again, and the air held the promise yet again of sunnier warm weather. It was early May, when one morning, Katie and I arrived at the yard to carry out the usual tasks. We were always the first ones there in the morning, so the job of unlocking everything fell to us. It was a bit of a faff as there was a sequence of unlocking feed stores, containers, etc., the keys of which were hidden strategically inside other feed stores, containers, etc.

On arriving at the first container, we realised the door was open and the hefty metal padlock was in pieces on the ground. We looked around, still a little bleary-eyed due to what to be fair was an ungodly hour, and still not quite daylight, and realised the door to the next container had also been opened. We looked beyond these and saw that the door to the Dutch barn housing the stables was swinging wide. Our hearts were in our mouths as we ran, imagining what an intruder could have done to our precious horses, if, in fact, the horses were all still there.

There's a constant threat of theft and social media often shares heartbreaking posts from distraught owners hoping to be reunited with horses and ponies that have been spirited away under cover of darkness, often never to be heard of again. In the few seconds it took to run to the stable block, it registered that the barn was silent. Normally, the horses all whinnied as they heard our car. It was with dread in our hearts that we looked over the 4-foot-high metal gates inside the big door expecting to see open doors, empty stables, or worse.

The first one to spot us, from his stable at the other end of the barn was, of course, Humbug, who whinnied joyfully to Katie. The relief that all twenty-one horses were there and unharmed was enormous and it was with shaky fingers I dialled the yard manager to let her know what had happened. Her first anxious question was, "Are the horses ok?" I could hear the relief in her voice as I explained that, although someone had obviously been inside the barn, nothing seemed to have been taken, including thankfully, the biscuit jar!

What would Humbug have done if that'd gone missing? With a sense of surrealism, we went about the morning routine—feeding, mucking out, and walking horses to the field amongst several police officers who were busy interviewing, fingerprinting, and photographing. It transpired that ours wasn't the only yard to have been targeted, but rather than the thieves looking for equestrian equipment or horses, they were apparently looking for tools and farm machinery which they could easily sell on.

The police checked our grainy CCTV footage and there's a chilling few minutes where a person wearing a hoodie opens the barn door, having first cut the lock, climbs over the gate and wanders around, actually looking over into some of the stables and stroking the bemused horses, before leaving again empty handed and with the horses unscathed. What might have been seen in that footage in other circumstances is unthinkable.

27

Winged Visitors

A horse can lend its rider the speed and strength he or she lacks, but the rider who is wise remembers it is no more than a loan!

Pam Brown

As we've already discussed, summer swallows were frequent visitors to the stables at the Yorkshire hill farm the horses first lived at and we were delighted when, during our first spring at the equestrian centre, we spotted a couple, then a couple more, then a whole abundance of them diving and swooping acrobatically over the barns.

Our lot weren't concerned at all by these delightful little birds swooping between their ears but some of the other horses turned into real divas, snorting and eye-rolling, stamping and reversing at speed, often refusing to enter their stables because of a tiny bird perched somewhere on a high ledge, not quite out of sight! A number of the horses when in their stables, inevitably, found themselves with a couple of nests overhead and it amused us to see those horses being led out to the fields in the mornings, already liberally spattered with tell-tale bird poo!

Slightly less charming were the wood pigeons, who spotted an opportunity to scavenge noisily for free food and lodgings in the barn. There appeared several nests in the rafters, each with a number of chicks squashed in, squeaking and squawking loudly. As the chicks outgrew the nests, the inevitable happened, and as it says in the song, 'They all rolled over, and one fell out'. Sadly, a couple of corpses were discovered in the early mornings when we opened up the barn and were quietly disposed of.

One victim of overcrowding, however, somehow miraculously survived the sky-dive and was found wandering around the barn, looking decidedly cocky, while his fretful mum flapped around and noisily reprimanded him for his risky behaviour. She desperately tried to persuade him to fly, presumably hoping he'd return to the nest, but he was having none of it. He'd tasted freedom and he was loving it! As always, with the confidence of youth, he didn't appreciate the perils of human feet, or indeed horses' hooves, and for several days had to be restrained for his own safety.

He was easily gathered up and placed in the ponies' stable once they were out in the field (Humbug had already shown an unhealthy interest in eating him!) and he settled himself down for a day of chilling, while his long-suffering mum flew back and forth keeping him well fed, flapping her wings to show him how flight was done, before going off to gossip with her friends, whose well-behaved chicks were still smugly ensconced in their nests.

Presumably, the mums had a good long chat about the difficulties of bringing up chicks to be good, law-abiding pigeons, and no doubt shook their heads in frustration at the roving delinquent! Inevitably, he was given a name; Pie, and was in serious danger of being cuddled to death by the staff and owners, but as his fluffy cuteness started to wear off, we all wondered how he was going to learn how to 'pigeon', bearing in mind his mum was rapidly becoming sick of his behaviour and was starting to wash her wings of him.

One morning, we almost didn't need to worry about this any longer as, although we could hear faint squawks, we couldn't find him anywhere. A couple of hours after us arriving, he was discovered in one of the stables, looking very sorry for himself, up to his knees (do pigeons have knees?) in a water bucket. He'd apparently fallen in and, judging by his very wet fluff, had been in there some time. It's likely the horse in that particular stable had simply drunk around him, but it suddenly dawned on us that he must be starting, albeit very incompetently, to fly!

Later that same day, he showed that he could manage to flap from the floor to the top of the stable doors and back, at which point he'd look around with a smirk on his beak as if to say, 'I might not be great at this yet, but I can still fly further than any of you!'. He had a point. Within a week, however, he'd mastered the art of flight and was soaring majestically around the barn, firing poo with alarming accuracy at both human and horse, and generally being a nuisance.

He quickly became pretty much indistinguishable from the other many, many pigeons around the place, but now and again, he'd pay a visit. We only knew it was him by the way he allowed us and the horses to walk right over the top of him without him batting a beady eye!

28

Bees!

Through the days of love and celebration and joy, and
through the dark days of mourning, the faithful horse has
been with us always.
Elizabeth Cotton

Come the summer and the horses enjoyed languishing in the fields during the heat of the long days. Every creature on the place seemed to be enjoying a slightly lazy pace of life and as far as the eye could see, were swishing tails, swooping swallows, snoozing sheep, waddling ducks…and bees! Yes, bees! One hot July day, as we went into the field the 'Little Chaps' still occupied, we noticed that a small swarm of bees had taken up residence on a fencepost just a couple of feet from the gate.

We were fascinated (from a respectful distance) and watched as the football-sized mass wriggled and writhed as more and more bees arrived and found their place within. The mass grew and evolved, mesmerisingly changing shape before our eyes, but as we suddenly heard hoofbeats coming closer, we realised Humbug had spotted Katie and was galloping enthusiastically across the field towards us…and towards the bees!

Katie rugby-tackled him, just managing to stop him sticking his nose into the mass that he'd heard buzzing. She deftly slipped on his headcollar and walked him over to collect Toby, who thankfully had the same cautionary idea as we'd had and was keeping a safe distance, eyes wide, nostrils twitching as he tried to work out what the moving thing was.

I sent a photo message to the yard manager warning her that she might want to find alternative accommodation for her own very valuable show jumper, who regularly spent time with the ponies in that little field. 'Bloody hell', came her immediate but not altogether helpful reply.

I turned to the internet for advice and read that bees often swarm in mid-summer if their home is disturbed by a careless human or blundering animal. It reassured me to read that within at most a couple of days, the scout bees that would've already been sent out on a recce will return armed with the details of a suitable des res and the whole lot of them will move on.

Almost a week later, however, they'd clearly not found anything they liked, be it the location, the room sizes, the schools, or they'd found some other issue with the properties they'd viewed, and they were looking rather too comfortable for my liking, still attached as they were to our fencepost. We decided to bring Henry, the landowner, to have a look. Rather unexpectedly, his round red-cheeked face lit up and he rubbed his hands together in glee! "Bloody marvellous!" He boomed happily.

What? Wait…that wasn't what we expected! It turned out, he'd 'acquired' some hives a couple of years previously and now simply needed to persuade some bees to move in. As he strode away, he shouted to us over his shoulder (he did this a lot, we'd noticed), "I'll make some calls and get the little buggers brought into the garden. We'll have honey in no time!"

A week later, with no sign of a relocation taking place any time soon, our bee population had multiplied massively. They'd obviously sent out the scouts, who reported back that actually, this was a very agreeable place to set up home and that they should also bring their relatives…by the thousand! We'd cautiously let the ponies back into the field and they seemed to be happy staying on the opposite side of the field, so we relaxed a little.

We'd become more confident around the swarm as the bees simply ignored us and went about their 'bizzzness', so we were happy to leave them bee… (Ok, I'll stop now) while we waited for Henry's 'man' to come and relocate them. One morning, as we turned the ponies out into the field, we caught a glimpse of something white and textured within the mass. A cautious closer inspection verified our suspicions—they were making honey and the white stuff we could see was the comb!

Having never watched bees in the process of doing their thing, we were fascinated at not only how quickly the comb was created but also how accurately identical the individual hexagonal chambers were. Each one glinted with golden, gloopy honey, which was starting to drip slowly onto the grass beneath. That evening, Humbug and Toby trotted across the field towards Katie when she called them. As he reached his favourite human, Humbug's attention was suddenly caught by something in the grass.

He swerved sideways and grabbed at a large piece of honeycomb that had apparently broken off the bottom of the structure. Suddenly, Humbug leapt backwards, still with gloopy honey dripping from his lips and began shaking his head from side to side. We can only assume that as he leaned forward to eat the honeycomb, his head had been too close to the bees on the bottom of the cluster and one of them must have taken exception to being tickled by furry Shetland ears and given him a zap!

It was a subdued Humbug that was led into the stables a few minutes later and a couple of people commented on his sad face and wonky ears! For reasons only known to himself, he felt the need to stick both ears out sideways, which admittedly is a skill that, until this point, I hadn't realised he possessed!

We couldn't find the site of an actual sting and he was a little reluctant to let us look too closely, so we dosed him up on antihistamines and gave him a carrot to cheer him up, while we dialled Henry's number to discuss the bees, again. He didn't answer my call (one of the downfalls of caller ID!), so I left a message asking if he'd mind popping round to the stables at some point to discuss transferring the bees, as one of his favourite Little Chaps had now been stung.

The following morning, Humbug was back to being his usual charming self, plus his ears were thankfully pointing upwards again but we felt it safest if he stayed in for the day. We know from experience that he has an internal tracker where food is concerned and we knew that if we turned him out, he'd hoof it straight back to the cluster of bees and dive straight in. A couple of the other owners had expressed an interest in the bees, but it's not the done thing to venture uninvited into each other's paddocks, stables and fields.

So, off I went armed with the shavings fork (with which I'd just mucked out two stables, Spirit's and the ponies') and scooped up what was left of the piece of honeycomb to bring back and show them. I wriggled it around on the fork as I tried to persuade a couple of reluctant bees to vacate it and was dismayed as it collected a couple of brown stains, remnants from the fork's most recent occupation. I placed the comb on the floor, as we all prodded and poked at it, and marvelled at its construction.

Slow, gloopy drops of honey were gathering into a small golden puddle on the concrete floor and little bits of gravel, along with pieces of straw and hay, ever-present at mucking-out time, had started already to stick to its surface.

Henry suddenly strode in and with his usual self-important air, parted the small crowd of onlookers. He leaned over the honeycomb, which was still oozing and dripping, picked it up in both hands and took a huge bite! We were staggered! He munched away, bits of comb, bugs, hay and honey gathering in his beard and he declared a muffled, "Mmm…bloody delicious!"

He spat out what looked suspiciously like a bit of bee and before taking his next bite, muttered, "I've got a chap coming along on Friday to move the bees into the garden... Probably best if the Little Chaps are out of the way."

He then turned his attention back to the drippy, oozy honeycomb in his hands. He grinned, rather revoltingly, through another huge mouthful, before striding away, appreciatively yummy noises emanating from him as he disappeared through the doors! The rest of us looked at each other in silence, before a loud shout of laughter filled the barn—who was going to be the one brave enough to mention that the comb had, only moments before he gobbled it up, been on my mucking-out fork gathering poo stains?

29

Out of Retirement!

A life without horses is like taking a breath without air.
Author unknown

The large indoor arena heralded much excitement when, on 31 December 2016, the builders finally finished! What a New Year's treat for us, particularly when we thought about the facilities at our old yard—an often-waterlogged outdoor school with broken lights, fences held together with string, and sharp rubble-like stones working their way up through the sand. We'd always dreamt of an indoor arena, but never expected we'd enjoy such decadence!

We were still at the yard quite late that night, the last ones there too (such is our social life!), so we sneaked the ponies from their stable and into the new arena. We turned on the many overhead lights and simply stood back in awe as we gazed at the huge, pristine space! We released the ponies, the first-ever equines to use the arena, and they galloped from one end to the other, over and over again, chasing each other, nipping necks, bucking, and generally having a ball!

Each time they reached the bottom end, they'd both turn and race each other back to us in a joyful flurry of sand, which they were kicking up from their little hooves! A great way to see in the New Year! They were panting as they reached us on their last lap and we suddenly realised that apart from one disastrous session of driving Humbug, during which he'd objected to being told he couldn't climb aboard a horsebox, reared and almost caused the cart to tip over, we'd hardly exercised them at all in the months we'd been there.

We tried to justify ourselves as we watched the ponies playing, by discussing the time we'd taken to school Rio, to get her and Spirit used to hacking out on unfamiliar tracks, we'd taken the ponies on walks along the many farm paths blah blah, but actually, we felt quite guilty for neglecting the fitness of the boys. We vowed to start an exercise regime for both of them, starting tomorrow—a good day for resolutions, 1 January!

The next morning, the stables were quiet as subdued owners and staff went about their duties with bleary and bloodshot eyes. We remembered our New Year's Resolution and, with admittedly a little less enthusiasm than we'd felt the night before, started to dig out Humbug's harness and bridle from the tack room. Due to its lack of use, the leather harness

178

had become dry and brittle; it desperately needed cleaning and oiling in order to make it supple again.

It was with some secret relief that we abandoned our mission for another day, justifying to ourselves that we'd feel terrible if Humbug's harness rubbed his delicate skin. A couple of weeks later, we roused ourselves again and got as far as actually putting the harness (freshly cleaned!) on him. His fur was so thick that the harness disappeared in his fluff, and it was difficult to fasten the many buckles without trapping and pulling his fur. Mission abandoned yet again!

However this prompted us to make a decision that we'd been skirting around for a while—clipping Humbug's fur completely off! Humbug's coat grows thick and fast, and there had been several mornings when we found he'd been sweating in the stable overnight. In previous years, we'd shaved his chest and armpits to give him some relief but we decided that now they were in a comparatively warm barn, so why not shave off the lot?

Katie was very much on board with this idea as she was generally the one who brushed the mud from his fur, so she found her set of clippers, plugged them in, and set to work. An hour later, Humbug was literally half the pony he'd previously been! Katie had left the fur on his legs as these would still be exposed to the elements when the ponies were out in the field and we giggled when someone commented on his furry 1980s-style legwarmers, but the rest of his coat was short, smart, and felt like expensive suede!

Several owners had been amused at how relaxed Humbug was during his clipping; he'd been tied up outside the stable but had immediately untied himself, so we let him stand quietly munching on a net of hay, totally unconcerned by the hefty pile of black and white fur collecting on the floor. Toby was watching with his head over the pony-sized stable door and was beginning to have a worried expression on his face, clearly wondering if he was next.

Toby's coat, although still very fluffy, is nowhere near as thick or coarse as Humbug's, so he doesn't suffer as much from overheating. Humbug's new sleek hairdo meant we could drive him again without the worry of him becoming sweaty, so the following weekend, once again the harness and bridle were fitted to him. Success! Momentarily…

We discovered on pulling out the cart from where it was stored that it had two flat tyres. Dammit! One of the perils of lack of use, I suppose. We went and found Henry to ask for his help and he told us that one of the guys who rented space in a barn to fix ex-army vehicles had a compressed air machine. We half-dragged, half-carried the surprisingly heavy cart round to him, and as we tried not to stare at the swirly black tattoo on his face and neck, the huge bear of a man told us that we needed new tyres as the inner tubes were…ahem…'broken'.

He offered to fix them both but explained that he'd need to remove the wheels and take them elsewhere for new inner tubes. We left them with him and went to unharness Humbug, yet again. A week later, the cart had shiny new tyres, so we excitedly planned to try yet again to do the driving thing…and Rio came down with colic.

Rio has always been a serial drama queen, so when she became unwell, it was initially difficult to ascertain just how much pain she was in. We noticed on the Saturday morning that she'd not done any poos in her stable during Friday night. She went out into the paddock as normal and, at the time, seemed her usual self, but a couple of hours later, she was rolling on the ground as she tried to alleviate the pain. Katie brought her back into the stable and gave her painkillers, which seemed initially to work, however, when they wore off, Rio seemed no better.

The vet was called, who administered fluids and pain relief, and left, confident that Rio would improve overnight. Katie stayed with her, but the following day, she was much worse and the vet was summoned yet again. She warned Katie that she thought the colic was possibly too severe for Rio to recover from and gave Katie the awful choice to make—keep trying or put Rio to sleep.

She admitted that if we could get her to the equine hospital, they could administer intravenous drugs, fluids, etc., and she may have a chance but didn't sound very hopeful. She warned Katie that this option could be very expensive. She suggested that Katie consider her options for a while and she went to stand a respectful distance away to give her the space to do just that. Katie was very quiet for a moment as she tearfully leaned her face against Rio's and stroked her neck.

She looked into her eyes, took a deep breath, and asked where we could hire a horse-transporter from. She wanted to give her horse every possible chance to recover.

A couple of hours later, friends at the yard had rallied round and found someone who could transport Rio in a lorry for the hour-and-a-half journey to the hospital. Katie and I followed in Katie's car and upon arrival, watched as they led a doped-up Rio into a large stable with deep bedding, fixed up the IV line for the drugs and fluids, and then gently but firmly suggested that we leave, so they could look after her. They very efficiently told Katie she could phone between certain times for an update and made sure they had Katie's number should they need to contact her.

It was with a feeling of stunned helplessness that I drove Katie's little car past the large barn which housed the various horsey patients and we saw Rio's grey face watching us leave. Katie was in no fit state to drive, so as she sat in the passenger seat of her car, she broke down and sobbed for her beloved horse.

The following day, we were told that a scan had shown a number of melanomas in Rio's gut, which had contributed to a huge blockage. She'd been diagnosed with these a couple of years earlier and we'd been aware of some developing on her head, as well as some smaller ones on her bottom, so this didn't come as a shock. It was very touch and go for a while but slowly over the next few days, Rio started to recover. The phone call telling us that she'd done a poo caused much celebration, and by the fifth day, she was declared well enough to come home again.

Katie had driven the 3-hour round trip to visit her every day and was relieved that she was coming back home again. She was painfully thin and desperately weak when we led her into her own stable and Katie wrapped her up in rugs to keep out the January chill. We'd been told to feed very little but often and to keep all her food very wet in order to ease its passage through her gut. She was reluctant to eat and even refused to drink for a while. We managed to syringe water into her mouth, lifting her head to prompt her to swallow.

This was a laborious procedure, bearing in mind that we had to get 5 litres of water into her every few hours. The following weeks were a nightmare. Rio was still losing weight and every rib protruded. Her neck looked too weak to support her head, she had no muscle tone, and she had no 'sparkle' to her. Katie was devastated and, for a while, it felt that Rio had simply given up. Katie admitted that she felt regular pangs of guilt at not having put her to sleep when it was suggested, but at the time, without having a crystal ball to advise us, we weren't aware of how the coming weeks might look.

It was many weeks before we started to notice some positive changes in Rio. Firstly, she started showing a slight interest in food and hay, and then she had a little spring in her step on the way to the paddock. Finally, she was well enough to be exercised gently in the outdoor school, and I believe that this was the turning point. Katie didn't ride her but loose-schooled her by giving commands from the ground. Suddenly, Rio was arching her skinny neck and striding out, actually enjoying herself!

It was a joy to watch, although as soon as other owners arrived, Katie quickly called an end to the session and took Rio back inside to put her rugs back on. We were very aware of how poor she still looked but there was more than a glimmer of hope on the horizon.

Months later, with summer just around the corner, Rio was looking like her old self and our thoughts turned yet again to driving Humbug. We were determined this time and set aside an evening when neither Katie nor I were working or had any other plans. We dug out the harness (ignoring the fact that it needed oiling again!) and as we clumsily fitted it to him, we realised it must have been five years since we'd driven him with any regularity. No wonder we were clumsy with the fitting of the harness.

Not only did we need reminding of how it all fitted together, but Humbug had changed shape in those years; he'd become a little fatter and a little less muscular, so the buckles needed adjusting to his new relaxed physique. Other owners wandered over to marvel at how cute he looked and we realised they thought of him and Toby just as cute fuzzy lawnmowers, not as the fit, athletic driving ponies we still had in our heads.

It was with quite a crowd of onlookers that we 'put Humbug to' his cart. His eyes had widened when he saw us wheeling it into the barn, but I wonder if he thought 'Here we go again' as we positioned it behind him. Suddenly, Humbug was no longer a retired child's pony, he was useful and important again. As he arched his neck and strutted out of the barn with Katie sitting proudly behind him, a small round of applause rippled around his gathered audience!

That first drive was done in the big outdoor arena, 100 metres across the carpark away from the stables, and which was usually used for showjumping lessons. The jumps were normally left up and it took some careful steering to ensure Humbug went around and between them without knocking the whole lot down. His admiring fans had followed us round there, and someone called out to Katie, pointing out that actually Humbug could go under most of the jump!

Katie had a big smile on her face as she negotiated the obstacles; a smile only equalled by the one on Humbug's face! He was thoroughly enjoying himself again and he puffed his chest out proudly and flicked his hooves as he walked and trotted around the arena. Excitement got the better of him a couple of times and he couldn't help but buck and squeal, which we know from experience can be a little disconcerting when you're sitting just inches from the back feet which suddenly hurtle towards you!

However, a stern word from Katie had him back under control and he worked hard for a half hour or so. At one point, I turned around and was amused to see several mobile phones pointing at him as people videoed his antics to put on social media sites. Later that evening, as I logged on to have a nosey at what friends and colleagues were up to, I was amused to see several videos of Humbug, each from a slightly different angle, as he strutted his stuff around the arena!

30
Aches and Pains

*Taking care of a horse is not just a duty, it's
a heartfelt responsibility.*
Author unknown

Humbug has always been an enthusiastic sunbather, and even
though he's had creaky joints for a while, he's usually been
able to alleviate any aches and pains during sunny weather by
sun worshipping, turning himself sideways on so that the sun
warms his achy joints. However, the summer after his return
to work, he came out of the field one day with a slight limp.
We didn't worry too much as he seemed to 'walk off'

whatever had bothered him and for a few days, he was absolutely fine.

Then, we realised the limp was back and it seemed to be on opposite corners, in his right front and left hind legs. We gave him a painkiller and again for a few days he was fine, before limping very slightly again. This on-and-off pattern continued for a few weeks but every time we saw the vet at the yard, typically Humbug was fine and rampaging around as usual. The vet admitted she was a little afraid of him, a statement which, when we considered the beasts she probably dealt with on a daily basis, made us scratch our heads a little!

One day, however, the vet saw him limping and after an 'arm's length' examination, which was all she was prepared to do without backup, she suggested that due to his age, Humbug probably had a touch of arthritis, and the recent damp weather was causing a bit more creaking than usual. She prescribed a small amount of pain relief to be added to his food on his worst days but to otherwise treat him as normal, turning him into the field and exercising him as usual.

Several weeks later, Humbug was clearly not happy and his limp was definitely worse. One day, we decided to take both ponies for a gentle walk as they'd been in the stable for a couple of days due to heavy rain. Just outside the stables, a huge puddle had formed. Katie knew Humbug would want to splash around and wallow in it, so she tried to keep him walking briskly through the shallowest part when, suddenly, there was a huge splash!

Humbug's legs had slid from underneath him and his head was underwater; he was blowing bubbles through his nostrils and had a comically shocked expression on his face! Poor Toby leapt sideways in alarm, clearly thinking that whatever underwater monster had tried to eat Humbug wasn't going to get Toby for its choice of dessert! Humbug regained his feet and dripping dirty water from his tummy, staggered to dry land, but we soon realised the tumble had made his limp much worse. He was now hobbling and seemed unable to bring the affected back leg underneath his body.

We decided that this had gone on for long enough and we rang the vet to make an appointment for x-rays.

We found somewhere locally to hire a horsebox and arranged to drive him the 50 miles to the equine hospital that had previously looked after Rio for his x-rays. The big day arrived, Humbug had been brushed and smartened up, his headcollar and fanciest red and blue tartan rug had been washed, and he was ready. Toby was coming along for moral support and it was on a cold, frosty day that Katie and I loaded them both into the hired lorry and set off.

When I say 'loaded', what actually happened is that Humbug spotted the open lorry at the far end of the car park, squealed in excitement, and dragged Katie across the frosty ground to clamber aboard! There was a partition along the inside of the lorry which we hadn't realised couldn't be removed. Normally, this is used in order to keep two full-size horses separated, therefore reducing the chances of them beating the bejeepers out of each other on the journey.

We set off with Humbug in one half and Toby in the other, each with their own haynet fastened securely. Predictably by the time we next looked, both ponies were in the same half, Humbug munching happily on the net we'd provided for Toby, with Toby squashed into the corner, looking glum.

Katie and I were quiet as we started the journey, both hoping silently that whatever was ailing Humbug was nothing that couldn't be fixed. As we had remarkably set off a few minutes earlier than planned (Katie is well-known for being late wherever she goes!), we decided that a fast-food breakfast was just what we needed to lift our spirits! It was with some amusement that we drove through the drive-through and alongside the order for coffee and breakfast muffins, we asked for ten bags of carrot sticks!

An hour later, Humbug and Toby were checking out their temporary accommodation and declared it to be up to standard. The shavings bed was deep, clean and comfortable, and there was a rack of good quality hay that if they stood on tip-hooves, they could just about reach! The staff were all friendly, competent, and efficient, and within minutes of us completing the admission and permission paperwork, they'd decided that Humbug looked like trouble and had injected him with a mild sedative in order to complete their examinations and x-rays safely.

It took effect almost immediately and he became very woozy, drooling slightly, eyes crossing as he still resolutely attempted to eat hay. Katie and I couldn't help but make the most of his incapacity and took the rare opportunity to cuddle and kiss him mercilessly! This was an almost unheard of treat; cuddling Humbug usually came with the risk of serious injury, and even in his heavily sedated, wobbly state, we could see his eyes narrowing as he clearly planned to get his revenge…just as soon as he could think straight!

5 minutes later, the x-rays showed advanced arthritis in both stifles and both hocks and also showed a very slight rotation of the pedal bone in one of his front hooves. In non-horsey speak, historic ailments and old age had definitely caught up and he would need some serious pain relief,

remedial foot trimming from our wonderful farrier, and very careful management for the rest of his life. We asked the staff a few minutes later how long the sedative would take to wear off as Humbug was showing no signs of coming around.

They suggested that in 5 minutes he'd be back to his usual self, so more quick cuddles were enjoyed (by us, not him!). Half an hour later, there was still no sign of him waking up and even Toby was starting to look concerned as his pal swayed in the stable, snoring dramatically, head down, drooling revoltingly, with his nose almost touching the floor! The staff kept coming along and peering at him through the stable windows, then going away again and we were starting to become a little worried.

An hour passed and a nurse suggested getting Humbug out into the fresh air, so we slowly guided him groggily towards the car park as his legs tried to plait themselves. We chuckled and told him he was like an old drunk staggering out of a pub on a Friday night, but he wasn't in any fit state to respond as he was still trying to work out which leg was on which corner!

Another half hour passed, and we'd seen a few horses arrive, be sedated, x-rayed, and watched as they trotted happily back into their horseboxes and lorries, having completely sobered up within minutes. We looked in dismay at our little drunk and wondered if he'd been faking it for the past hour and a half just for the attention. Katie retrieved a leftover carrot stick from the lorry and waved it under his nose. He barely reacted! Nope, this wasn't him faking anything, he was absolutely sozzled!

Time went on and on, and we started to wonder what time the clinic closed, but eventually, Humbug started to lift his head and look around in surprise at his surroundings. He clearly had no recollection of where he was, or why, and even seemed surprised to see Toby, who by this time was taking a break from the marathon trek around the carpark and was eating hay in the lorry.

They whinnied to each other and it was with some relief that 15 minutes later, Katie allowed herself to be dragged up the ramp into the vehicle by Humbug who, by now, had a serious case of the munchies! I'm surprised he didn't demand to stop by a kebab shop on the way home!

A couple of days later, we saw Henry, who asked how the Little Chap was doing. We explained that Humbug would need careful daily management and pain relief on and off for the rest of his life and that his international showjumping days were probably behind him. Henry glossed over my poor attempt at humour but did suggest that instead of the boys hobbling around the now muddy little field that he'd kindly provided, how about letting them wander around an unused lunging pen on wet days?

This for us was a great idea as washing the sticky clay mud off Humbug's legs day after day couldn't have helped his arthritis. We tried them in the pen the following day and they loved it! The advantage for the ponies was that the pen was right next to where owners and visitors parked their cars, meaning that there was the possibility of treats from every single person who arrived! Humbug exploited this to the max, resting his chin on the wooden fence, fluttering his eyelashes, and turning up the cute.

We considered having a sign made, advising that Humbug might not actually be starving to death as he would have his audience believe and that feeding him would be a serious risk to fingers. However, as often happens when people meet Humbug, his charm soon wore off and he was given a wide berth.

This makeshift paddock, or pony-playpen as it came to be known, was used ever since. Even on cold winter's days, the boys enjoyed a few hours tootling around in there with haynets and toys, wearing their rugs, and came back in clean and dry. Horses and ponies on some kind of rehabilitation from illness or injury have gone in there with them, their owners confident that they're in safe hooves. Humbug and Toby are excellent hosts and welcome everyone into their playpen, willing to share hay and water without a hint of jealousy.

A regular visitor was a moody, hormonal mare called Cassie, who has in the past been very aggressive towards other horses but paradoxically hates being without company. She couldn't be put with other horses in fields or paddocks as she would attack them, but if she was on her own, she would escape to look for company...who she would then attack! Bearing in mind the very laid-back, kind, and friendly nature of both Humbug and Toby, we'd already cautiously floated the idea of putting Cassie in the paddock with them.

I felt confident that even if she showed some aggression towards them, they wouldn't fight back, which would hopefully take the wind out of her sails. A date was set for the meeting a week or so ahead and every night beforehand, we walked Humbug and Toby over to Cassie while she was in her stable. This wasn't ideal as, like many mares, she was quite territorial and also very protective of her haynet, but as time went on, she started to show less aggression towards them.

Instead of flinging herself at the door, teeth bared and ears pinned flat, she started to give them an 'Oh, it's just them again' kind of look. Finally, a couple of nights before the big day, she reached out with her muzzle, ears forward, a friendly look about her face, and briefly touched noses with Humbug. Success! Two days later, on a warm, sunny day, with breath held, we cautiously let Cassie into the playpen with the ponies.

The boys looked up from eating, regarded Cassie with very little interest, and went back to stuffing their faces. Cassie trotted around the unfamiliar area, tossed her head, shook her mane, and broke into a canter towards where the boys were munching. She skidded to a halt, put her head down, and ate hay alongside them! Phew… We realised, Cassie's owner, Katie, and I that we'd each been holding our breath for the past few minutes and were starting to become lightheaded!

We laughed in relief as the adrenaline started to recede and, after a few more minutes of watching very little activity, we shut the gate and left them to it. It was with some pangs of nerves that we went back for a look at them 15 minutes later, wondering what carnage we'd find, but again, they were all sunbathing happily, tails swishing in the weak winter sunshine. She either hadn't noticed that under the fluff there were actual ponies, or maybe she was hatching a grand plan to fatten them up to eat later!

Or maybe, just maybe, Humbug and Toby had worked their charm and she actually quite liked their company. Either way, they were a strange little family, slightly dysfunctional, but it seemed to work for them.

It was eventually decided that Cassie could go back out into the field for some time on the grass. However, she clearly wasn't happy and stood for hours at the gate shouting. She started to lose weight as she refused to leave the gate to graze, but none of the other owners were prepared to risk their horses in the field with her, so it was decided that she could join the boys in the pen some days and the others she'd have to stay in her stable.

Humbug had shown Cassie's owner his true colours when he led her to believe she could get through the gate without him escaping! We've warned everyone who comes into contact with the boys of Humbug's escapology pursuits but he'd obviously lulled her into a completely false sense of behaving! She was bringing the little mare in for the night and, as the weather was starting to turn wintery, she sent me a text asking if I'd like the boys putting in their stable too. I was at work, and wouldn't be there for another couple of hours or so, and I sent a message back accepting her kind offer, but warning that Humbug bites, pointing out his liking for thigh-flesh, and advising that he will escape given half a chance.

40 minutes later, a very apologetic text came, which ended with the words, 'I didn't realise he could run so fast or dodge so well!'. Humbug had waited until she was bending down to put his headcollar on and he suddenly set off at a gallop through the slightly open gate. Apparently, it took several people, a couple of farmers on tractors, and a bucket of food to tempt him into being caught! Cassie's owner said afterwards that she never realised that Humbug could actually grin…!

31
The Beast from the East

*The horse, with beauty unsurpassed, strength immeasurable,
and grace unlike any other, still remains humble enough to
carry a man upon his back.*
Amber Senti

The very start of 2018 was a hard one for horse owners. Or maybe it was only hard for horse owners keeping said horses on our yard. It became apparent the barn must have been converted to stables during a warm summer, if the uninsulated water pipes, bare metal roof, and smooth concrete floor were anything to go by!

The water froze in the pipes, sleety rain came through the roof, black ice seemed ever-present in the carpark, through which we precariously walked our horses to their paddocks, and every surface in the stables was regularly covered in a layer of frost. Every horse took on a dragonesque appearance as plumes of steamy breath wafted upwards towards the pigeons.

The end of February saw the arrival of Anticyclone Hartmut or the 'Beast from the East'; weather coming directly from Siberia which brought with it the first serious snow of the winter, dropping the already sub-zero temperatures even further, freezing everything solid, and for several days, our cars were completely snowed in. Our horses, therefore, had to be entrusted to the dedicated yard staff, a couple of whom walked from their homes in the next village and worked tirelessly throughout the day to make sure their charges had food, hay, bedding, and adequate rugs.

Fresh water, however, was a different matter. The whole farm was completely frozen up and there wasn't a drop of liquid water anywhere. It's easy to fill a kettle with a couple of handfuls of snow if it's half a dozen chickens you're trying to provide with a warm drink, but when it's upwards of, at this point, twenty-five horses all needing up to 12 gallons of water every day, it's a different matter!

Henry was consulted by the yard manager, but Henry had other pressing issues; his many, many sheep had collectively decided that two feet of snow, gale force winds, and wind-chill temperatures reaching as low as −15 degrees C were the perfect conditions to start lambing!

Once he'd built a makeshift pen in the hay barn using bales of straw, an old gate and bits of string (are farmers born knowing how to do this?), he rounded up a number of ewes and their shivering lambs, deposited them in their temporary accommodation, and several hours after he'd been called upon, turned his attention to our water, or lack of it. Someone was despatched in a pick-up truck to purchase an enormous container which sat inside a protective metal cage arrangement.

Henry then managed to syphon enough water from the nearby river to fill it. He carried it, rather sloshily, into the barn on the front forks of his little tractor and placed it at the top end near where the ponies' stable was. And drove away! Nobody knew how to get the water out and they ran after him, shouting! Clearly, though, he had 'a plan', as finally he came back, bringing with him a long length of 3" diameter black rubber hose, and a hand pump!

The pump was fitted to an attachment on top of the container, a person of agile build was assigned the task of climbing on top and working the pump, and hey presto! We had water! But we had a total of twenty-five horses, each one needing at least two large tubs of water per 24 hours, and each tub took approximately 5 minutes to fill. This wasn't a quick job, bearing in mind the majority of owners (including us) were completely snowed in, the staff had a mammoth task on their work-roughened, chapped and frozen hands.

Not only did they have to provide water for each horse, but they also had to muck each one out, pushing a heavy wheelbarrow up the icy slope to the muckheap after cleaning out each stable, fill and carry haynets, mix each individual feed, change rugs, and check each horse over before moving on to the next one. And just three people were doing this before shutting the doors for the night and, as they'd had to walk in, walk back home again.

We owe a massive debt of gratitude to each of those lovely, hardworking, dedicated members of staff who stepped in and made sure our horses were fed, watered, warm, and happy.

The following day, the weather was even worse. The snow had continued overnight and was over a foot thick on the lane where we live. Again, we were forced to contact the yard and reluctantly hand over the care of Spirit, Rio, Humbug, and Toby to the staff. The message came back, 'We'll do what we can, but the water container froze overnight and we now have a block of ice the size of a small shed!'.

It was another couple of days before a friendly farmer with a tractor and snowplough dug out our village streets and the steep hills that we so far hadn't dared brave. We slithered cautiously in Katie's car down the hills to the main road and from there, we finally made our careful way to the equestrian centre to see our horses. Our journey was an eye-opener; drifts higher than the roof of the car lined many of the roads and huge piles of dirty brown snow and ice were left by snowploughs at intervals along our route.

A lorry partially blocked one of the roads, having skidded and ended up almost on its side, toppling partway down a ditch. We slowed down and crept carefully past, winding the window down to make sure the driver was ok. He had a shovel and was pointlessly digging snow from around his many, huge tyres. How he was planning to put the lorry back on its wheels, I have no idea!

We parked just inside the gateway, rather than risk driving down the track, and as we walked through the still-thick snow, we wondered whether our horses would be happy to see us, or if they'd give us the cold shoulder for abandoning them.

Humbug must have ears like a bat, as even before we were in sight of the barn, he'd heard Katie's voice and we could hear him shouting to her! He was pawing frantically at the stable door, barging and biting Toby to get him out of the way as Katie hurried towards them, giving Rio just a quick pat and a kiss on the nose as she went past her. Humbug was beside himself with joy that his favourite human had arrived and trotted in circles around the stable, each time coming back to where Katie was standing, to bite her on the legs (his own unique version of a love bite!) as she fussed and cuddled him.

Eventually, Katie, out of self-preservation, came out of the stable and went next door to further check on Rio, whose welcome, it has to be said, was a little lukewarm compared to Humbug's. Katie's main man loudly demanded more attention, so she quickly slipped on his headcollar and took him out for a play in the snow.

He sunk to his knees almost as soon as he was outdoors and, not caring that he was blocking the way for humans with loaded wheelbarrows, he rolled around ecstatically in the cold, deep snow, waving his feet in the air and 'scrimmying' to make sure every bit of him was covered! Finally satisfied, he scrambled to his feet, farted loudly, coughed, and bit Katie on the leg! He was happy again!

Katie was later told by the staff that he was fine the first day, a little subdued on the second, but by the third day when staff arrived, he was laid in his bed, looking utterly dejected and was showing little interest in anything, even food. They tried to tempt him with treats and cough medicine from the bottle, one of his favourite things, to no avail. The boy was miserable, missing his favourite human, and not liking that his routine had changed.

Katie and I discussed that when she has been on holiday, or away on training, both Annie and I have still been around to jolly Humbug along. 3 days without any of us had taken its toll on him and I worry what would happen to him if we went on a family holiday, for instance. I suppose it's a good thing I can't afford exotic holidays in the sun, but I bet there aren't many parents who, when their children are grown and lead independent lives, pass up the opportunity to enjoy a weekend break away because the Shetland pony will sulk!

32
On the Move Again

A horse gallops with his lungs, perseveres with his heart,
and wins with his character.
Tesio

That year's spring had brought the 'Beast from the East' in terms of weather, but it also brought a worrying financial issue. A brand-new yard manager, who had bought the business from the original owner just a few weeks before, had clearly had far too long to sit at home with her calculator while her dedicated staff walked to the yard to do the work.

She decided that as we were the only owners on DIY livery, we were a financial burden and she could earn far more money for our stables by either taking on full liveries in our place or charging us more money for our horses to continue living there. I received a text message advising me that the yard would no longer be offering DIY livery and if we wanted to keep our horses there, we would be charged the same rate as the owners whose horses were looked after by the staff.

This meant our monthly fee would almost double, and after a bit of calculating, I realised that Spirit's livery alone would, in a couple of weeks, be exactly twice as much per month what I paid for my mortgage! Bearing in mind her stable was 12 feet x 12 feet, per square foot it would cost... No, I resolutely refused to do the maths!

I asked the yard manager if we could discuss this face to face, bearing in mind our horses were absolutely no work-burden to the staff at all, as apart from the few snow days, we did everything ourselves, but I was told the decision was already made and our fee would increase at the next pay date, less than 2 weeks away. I did the sums and realised there was simply no way we could afford to stay there any longer on the new price structure; there just wasn't enough money available.

With sinking hearts, we started the process of looking for somewhere else for our horses to live, trying to ignore the fact that we would no longer be a part of the fantastic livery family that we had been embraced within during the past 18 months. Frantic phone calls were made to horsey friends, numbers were passed on, messages were left... Nowhere had enough stables available, particularly as we were trying to find somewhere that would accept Shetlands, which most yards won't.

Carrie, a friend of ours from many years ago, was half-heartedly looking to move her horse from his current yard but was hoping for a simple field with a shelter, rather than a yard with stables and an arena, which was the least we were hoping to find. We discussed how great it would be if we could all move somewhere together. But where?

We were losing all hope of ever finding somewhere and had even discussed the possibility of separating them (and we really didn't want to think too hard about this option), keeping the boys where they were and finding somewhere else for the girls, or letting Carrie take the ponies as companions for her horse if she found a field big enough for them.

It was with an increasing sense of desperation that I searched every internet and social media site to no avail, rang every single farmer within a 10-mile radius and left messages at every livery yard in the area, each time being told the same—sorry, but no. I visited the feed merchant during the week and as I waited my turn at the counter, I was idly browsing through the handwritten postcards advertising alpaca shearing and chickens for sale, when hidden amongst them was a small scrap of paper, with the words I'd been longing to see: 'DIY Livery Available'.

I quickly swiped it from the board and once I'd paid for my purchases, I ran out to my car, hands trembling as I dialled the number.

'Your call cannot be taken at the moment' was the automated phrase that had me swearing violently. I left a garbled, frantic message trying to explain that I had four horses, two of which share a stable, plus a friend who has one, all of which would like to come; the two girls would share a field, the ponies needed restricted grazing, but we had our own fencing; we'd like to be able to help our friend when she needed it (some yards won't allow this). Even to my ears, it sounded ridiculous, desperate and confusing. I gave up and asked the recipient of my message to ring me when they got a chance. And I waited. And waited.

A day later I tried again, only to be met, frustratingly, with the same message. A text was painstakingly composed and finally sent, which I think made a little more sense, and within minutes a reply came! The yard owner apologised for the poor signal and invited us to go for a look around and discuss further. We turned up the next day at the small farm which, it turned out, is situated on the hill opposite the one we live on! If we were to chop down a small thicket of trees in between, we would have been able to wave at Humbug from Katie's bedroom window!

So, there we were, at the arranged time, bundled up in thick coats, woolly hats, scarves, gloves, and boots, hoping to keep out the driving snow which had returned with a vengeance, hardly daring to ask if she'd allow us to bring the ponies.

The yard owner explained that a lady had arranged to move her four horses to the yard the previous weekend but had changed her mind at the last minute, so if we wanted the stables, we could move all of them whenever we wanted.

She showed us a block of four stables opposite the house, one occupied by a lovely black heavyweight cob, whose owner has since become a trusted friend, and a small barn containing two further stables housing her own horses, a lovely grey hunter and an elderly chestnut gelding. Next to this was another block with a further couple of stables, inside one of which was a pony, who was apparently there to be sold and would soon be moving on.

We had a look at the fields, which were sloping steeply towards a busy road; not ideal but we weren't in a position to be fussy. There was a small shabby arena with floodlights for the dark nights and hay was included in the price. Perfect! We quickly arranged to move the following week, snow permitting, and despite the place being nothing like as smart as our current yard, we breathed sighs of relief that we'd found somewhere not only that we could afford, but that would allow the boys to live there, and was within a couple of miles of home.

The owner, a lady called Joan, seemed lovely and was happy for us to festoon her fields with our electric fencing in order to contain the ponies. There was even enough room for our friend Carrie's horse, Dexter!

During our last couple of weeks at the yard, there was controversy around the increased charges and senseless changes the yard manager was implementing. She had, however, decided that the yard's security needed to be increased, not a bad idea on paper, and arranged for an automatic gate to be installed at the very top of the long driveway. Great, or so we thought.

What she also implemented was an automatic sliding closure and locking mechanism, which was set to lock at 6.30 pm, which was half an hour after her staff finished work. Unfortunately, as we could only visit the yard after we finished work, by the time 6.30 came around, we were often still bringing our horses in for the night, bedding down and feeding them, or exercising them in the indoor school.

It meant that we had to keep a close eye on the time and there were too many evenings that saw us racing up the drive in our car, wide-eyed and determined to get through the gap before the gate closed '1990s Crystal Maze' style, thus locking us in for the night.

Assuming we made it through the gate, our car would then be on the side of a busy road and we'd have to climb over the gate, walk back down the drive, finish off what we were doing (occasionally having left Spirit or Rio tacked up in the stable, puzzled at the interruption to the exercise session), and then we'd have to walk back up the drive again at the end of the night, scramble over the high gate hoping the car was still in one piece.

This was all 'best case scenario' though, and the alternative ending was that we missed the 6.30 pm lock-in and had to phone the yard manager and plead with her to do whatever jiggery-pokery on her control settings to release us. She had caller ID, and didn't like us much, so it was all very hit-and-miss as to whether she'd answer. A couple of times we had to phone someone to pick us up at the top of the drive and deliver us back to the yard the next morning.

She then decided every horse owner had to use shavings instead of straw for the beds, and that they must purchase the shavings from her, at a vastly inflated price than we'd all been paying thus far. Our shredded paper bedding bales had for years cost approximately £4 each, and we'd found a supplier of the normally more expensive wood shavings who could supply in bulk at the same price. The yard manager was charging £7.50 each!

Several owners contested this and were advised that there was no alternative; accept it or leave the yard. She also introduced increased livery prices across the board and it soon became apparent that other owners were, like us, starting to look elsewhere. However, as soon as the YM found this out, she confronted the ones who were looking and gave them a month's notice. I took some smug delight in telling the YM that we would be leaving and chose to ignore her blatantly insincere, "Oh, what a shame, we'll really miss you! Come back any time, you'll be more than welcome."

As time went on, it became clear that we weren't the only ones moving. In total, seven of the twenty-one horses moved on the weekend that we left, some to yards many miles away, which indicates how desperate some owners had become. Another four left the following week; a massive percentage of previously happy people pushed out by greed.

A friend from the yard, Clara, who was another of the leavers, offered to transport Spirit and Rio for us in her little silver lorry, which was affectionately known as Sylvia. Bearing in mind how terribly Spirit loaded last time, we decided to let her do it. I asked our old friend Carrie's husband, John, if he'd help us move the ponies, the bedding, and all the equipment early the following morning in their trailer, and suddenly, everything was arranged.

On the big day, Humbug and Toby trotted happily up the ramp of the trailer and disembarked just a few minutes later in their new home. They actually looked a little disappointed that their road trip wasn't a longer one, but a few carrots cheered them up as they waited for their big sisters to join them. There was a lot of activity at the equestrian centre that day; lots of people were packing, lorries and trailers were being loaded up with various horses, and owners were hugging and promising to keep in touch.

Interestingly, the yard manager was nowhere to be seen. Suddenly, almost without us realising, Spirit was loaded and ready to go. Wow! Where was our friend Clara when we'd moved TO the yard 18 months earlier? 10 short minutes later, Spirit walked happily off the lorry and into her new stable, looking around at her new home with interest. Just half an hour later, Rio joined her. Compared to the move we'd undertaken 18 months ago, this one had been a doddle!

The weather on moving day had been incredibly kind, bearing in mind the sub-zero battering we'd endured for what felt like months. We'd loaded and unloaded everyone in unseasonal sunshine; we'd even been brave enough to take off our coats as we hung up rugs and positioned feed bins in the little storage room we'd been allocated. Humbug and Toby stood tied very securely to the rings outside their new stable and warmed their bottoms in the sunshine as we put down shavings to make their beds.

We decided that as the weather had clearly turned a positive corner, we'd wait until tomorrow to find the fencing stakes, tape, and electric box which we'd need to make the boys a secure paddock. How wrong this decision was! 'Tomorrow' dawned with a fresh covering of snow, strong winds, −8 temperatures, and roads that were rapidly becoming impassable…again! We were desperate to visit the new yard to make sure our horses had been ok overnight, but how would we get there?

It was becoming clear that we needed to walk. Oh well, at least this yard was only a couple of miles away, rather than the 8 miles we travelled every day to get to the equestrian centre! At 7 am, we togged up in several layers of clothing, wellies, extra socks, scarves, woolly hats, gloves—Katie even had earmuffs on—and we set off to trek down the hill to the village, and back up the other side. We'd been walking for about 10 minutes and felt intrepid when Carrie rang us to ask if we wanted a lift as she was going to try the journey in her very capable 4x4 vehicle.

Sod being intrepid; her car had very efficient heaters! 5 minutes later, we were ensconced in comfy leather seats with built-in bum warmers, singing along to the radio, the heater blasting our cold faces with hot air, and we even shared some sweeties left behind by Carrie's daughter! The car admittedly struggled slightly on the steeper icy hills and there were a few bum-clenching, sharp-intake-of-breath moments when other drivers skidded wide-eyed towards us, but on the whole, we made the journey unscathed.

It was with some reluctance a few minutes later that we re-gloved, re-hatted, and left the luxuriously warm sanctuary of the comfortable 4x4, braced ourselves and slithered together down the steep driveway of the little farm. However, the welcoming whinnies of our cosy, happy horses who were watching us arrive made the cold and the journey worthwhile. It was clear, as the settling snow was building, that today was not going to be the day to make a pony paddock.

We did, however, rug everyone up and turned them into the little arena for a leg stretch while we mucked out the stables and filled haynets. It took maybe a minute for Humbug to find an escape route! He didn't even bother to wait until our backs were turned and we watched in dismay as he climbed a low wall, scrambled up a slope, ducked expertly under a length of electric fencing, and into the field above the arena.

Watched jealously by the others, he strutted smugly as he found a flattish area, scraped the snow with his hoof in order to make a suitable rolling spot, and sunk to his knees to indulge. We realised that we didn't know whether the field had Humbug-proof fences and as we didn't want him getting out onto the road or into neighbouring properties, we abandoned the mucking-out and all set about catching him.

He thought this was a splendid game and galloped enthusiastically from one end of the field to the other, little hairy legs a blur, plumes of steamy breath flying from his nostrils, flurries of snow in his wake. He hadn't, however, accounted for the field being icy underneath the covering of fresh snow and his face registered comic horror as he suddenly realised a moment too late that his brakes weren't working! He skidded with a crash into the wooden perimeter fencing and, in the moments it took for him to regain his composure, Katie quickly ran over and put on his headcollar.

As she was leading him to the gate, we heard a shout from the upstairs window of the farmhouse, "What have I let myself in for, letting you bring bloody Shetlands here?"

Thankfully, the yard owner, Joan, was more amused than annoyed, and as she made her way outside a few minutes later, bundled up in hat, coat, scarf, wellies, and gloves, brandishing very welcome mugs of steaming coffee, followed by a massive German shepherd and a hugely fat labrador, she fondly remembered the Shetlands of her own youth and more recently those of her daughter's.

We felt cautiously confident that some of Humbug's 'quirks' would be overlooked bearing in mind she had some experience of Shetlands, but we made a resolution to create a suitable pony pen just as soon as the ground thawed slightly.

We had a few difficult weeks of snow, ice, hail, and rain before the ground finally softened up enough to put the horses out in the fields. The paddock allocated to Humbug and Toby was, apart from the steepness and the busy road at the bottom, almost ideal. We decided to section it off so they didn't guzzle too much grass, and we realised at that point that we'd left most of our fencing posts at the equestrian centre. None of us felt inclined to go grovelling back to ask the unpleasant yard manager for them, so we managed with what we had.

Two sides of the paddock had post-and-rail fencing anyway, so we only had to fence off the remaining two sides. Spirit and Rio had been allocated the paddock next door, so we put Shetland height fencing along that side to stop the boys from escaping through to their bit, and along the top edge where the path to the paddocks ran. We also fashioned a gate from the electric tape as the existing wooden sliding bars we knew would pose little challenge for Humbug.

We positioned the control panel immediately next to the gate, in the hopes that anyone who might bring the boys in remembered to turn off the electricity before opening it!

With some relief, we finally released the ponies into their new field. They trotted happily to the bottom and had a look through the sturdy wooden fence at the traffic whizzing past, before turning and gazing in dismay at the steep slope that they would have to hike back up! They scrambled part of the way up the muddy, still slippery field, gave up, and having had a quick check that the fence was on (of course it was!), they turned their attention to the grass.

We'd split their field in half, and obviously, they assumed the fenced-off part had much tastier grass than the bit they were in. An hour later, they'd munched a track which ran along the length of the fence as they got as close as they could to what they perceived to be the 'good stuff'!

After what had felt like a long, long winter, spring eventually arrived. We settled into a routine of me going up to the yard in a morning and turning everyone out, doing some of the stable jobs, and then going off to work, having called back home first to wash away whatever stains Humbug had coated me with. Then, in the evenings, Katie and I would go back up together to bring everyone back in. She would exercise Spirit and Rio in the little arena, then we'd finish the jobs together and leave for the night.

I'd not ridden Spirit in a few months as I needed a hip replacement due to advanced osteoarthritis, and although I could get around, I was in a lot of pain negotiating the steep hills at the new yard and didn't feel able to ride safely. However, the daily routine we'd carved out fitted in well with both Katie's waitressing job in a local restaurant and my job for the city council, and also with Katie's studying; she was by now studying Interior Architecture and Design at Sheffield Hallam University.

Annie was also a waitress but in a popular city-centre restaurant and spent much of her free time at her boyfriend's house. She would occasionally show up at the yard, enjoy cuddles with a very obliging Toby, take a whole bunch of selfies with him, and disappear again! Spring turned gradually into summer, Katie readied herself for a long, long holiday from university, Annie and a friend went off travelling around Europe, and the hip replacement operation that I'd needed for such a long time was suddenly scheduled!

I had a couple of weeks of dreading it, sorting out things at work, and worrying about what would happen regarding the

212

horses, and then the big day arrived! Nerves kicked in (I'd never had an operation before) and as Katie and I sat in the car park of the hospital, I made up my mind that I couldn't go through with it.

"Fine, I'll take you back home," Katie said as she started the car, "but you know you'll never ride Spirit again, don't you?"

She knew just the right thing to say. Within minutes of walking nervously through the hospital doors, I was gowned up and making my way trembling to the operating theatre! It turned out the staff realised just by looking at me that I was a flight risk and thought they'd better do my operation before I made my escape. I stayed in the hospital a few days following the operation and then was sent home on crutches to recover, with strict instructions from the surgeon to stay away from horses for a while. Yeah, right; like that was ever going to happen!

A week passed, but that was all I could manage and I talked Katie into taking me to see Spirit. Joan, the yard owner, welcomed me with a big hug as we arrived, brought out a comfy chair for me to sit in, propped my crutches against the wall, and then proceeded to tell me how hard Katie had worked during my absence keeping the whole horse routine going. I'd had no doubts at all that Katie would be fine doing everything, even while juggling her shifts in the restaurant, but it's great when someone else tells you how wonderful your kids are!

Katie had been on her way from the field and was walking into the yard with Spirit and Rio while Joan was singing her praises, and I was delighted but not surprised to see Spirit looking happy and healthy. She seemed pleased to see me again too, if a little puzzled as to why I was in a comfy chair, but overlooked that in favour of enjoying the banana I'd brought her (her favourite thing!). Katie had gone back down to the fields to bring up Humbug and Toby, and subconsciously, Joan stood protectively in front of me.

She knew Humbug well by this point. I was delighted to see the boys but Humbug simply gave me little more than a cursory glance as he followed Katie into the stable. Talk about being underwhelmed! Despite Humbug's lukewarm welcome, it was wonderful to be out in the summer sunshine, listening to the hum of the bees, the call of the birds and the farts of the horses! I'd missed them all so much and was looking forward to being back to full fitness so I could enjoy their company again.

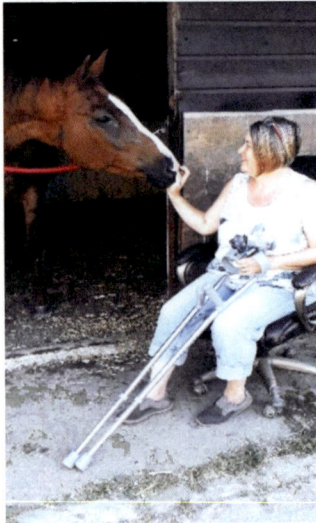

33
A Sad Day

To place your horse's need for you to let him leave his failing body above your need to keep him with you, that is the greatest and purest love.
Author unknown

Almost exactly a year later, my hip fully healed and feeling great, we were back to our original routine of splitting the daily chores between Katie and me. Her 4 long years at university were drawing to a close, final projects were being tweaked to perfection, and she was starting to seriously think about her future, looking for jobs and thinking about how to pay off the huge student loan.

I noticed one morning that Rio wasn't her usual self and rang Katie to ask her to have a closer look at her later that day. We noticed over the next few days that Rio's stomach was becoming bloated and hard, like a drum. We also realised that she was struggling to pass water, and the vet, after a couple of home visits, decided she was worried enough about her to schedule an in-depth ultrasound scan so that we could assess what was going on.

The appointment was made, the lorry booked, and it was with growing feelings of dread that we arranged to drive Rio on the 50-mile journey. She'd deteriorated over the week and was clearly very unwell. It was a miserable, grey, rainy morning when we loaded Rio into the hired lorry. She looked back at Spirit who'd been left in the stable and they simply gazed quietly at each other for a few moments before we drove away.

I think, looking back, we all knew the outcome of the day, and we (Katie, Annie, and I) drove almost silently the journey we'd come to know too well. An hour after we arrived, investigations revealed that Rio had developed a neurological condition that was preventing messages from her brain from reaching her bladder, which was as a result no longer able to empty and had enlarged over the week to massive proportions. The same vet who'd nursed Rio through colic a few years before now had to break the devastating news to Katie that her beloved mare would not recover from this condition.

While trying to be business-like and efficient, the vet, a horse owner herself, was able to be sympathetic to Katie and understanding of her grief. Katie was beside herself but was allowed as long as she needed to say goodbye to Rio, who having been administered a large dose of pain relief, was looking much more comfortable. Katie didn't want Rio to pick up on her grief and tried her very best to be 'normal' around her for the remaining time they had together.

It is a testament to Katie's strength of character and the love she had for Rio that she was able to go into the stable with her to play the games and do the tricks that had always been part of Rio's day. It's comforting to know that Rio's final minutes were spent free of pain, enjoying Katie's company, being told what a good girl she was, and earning carrots for playing the familiar games she'd always enjoyed.

The journey home was simply terrible. I'd sent a message to Joan, letting her know that Rio had been put to sleep, as I didn't want to have that conversation when we arrived back at the yard without her. It seemed barely believable that only a couple of weeks earlier, Rio had been her usual quirky, funny self, racing around the field with Spirit, and now we were driving an empty lorry home from the hospital.

The weather had turned even worse and as we negotiated the dismal, grey motorway in torrential rain, Katie curled up on the seat at the side of me and sobbed, and there was absolutely nothing Annie or I could do to help her.

34
Closer to Home

A good horseman can hear his horse speak to him. A great horseman can hear his horse whisper.
Author unknown

Spirit was desperately upset by Rio's death and stopped eating. For 3 weeks, she relentlessly patrolled the perimeter of the field, almost as though she was looking for her over the fences. She would look intently up the drive and whinny loudly every time she came into the yard. I realised that her last sighting of Rio was as she was driven in the lorry up the drive and she was looking for her. It was heartbreaking to witness her grief and be unable to explain it to her.

Anyone who thinks animals are incapable of complex emotions should have taken a look at Spirit in those weeks, clearly grieving for her friend and feeling lost and alone. I tried every different food I could think of to try to entice her into eating, as she was losing weight and condition, but nothing tempted her. She even refused bananas, her favourite treat. Then one day, as she was walking past the ponies' stable, she reached in and grabbed a mouthful of hay from their net!

I stood with her for a few minutes as she helped herself to the ponies' hay, while Humbug and Toby politely stood back and allowed her to eat. It wasn't an ideal arrangement, but at least she was eating.

Slowly over the next few weeks, Spirit seemed to come to terms with her loss and started to show a little interest in food again. She still patrolled the field and seemed to not like being in there alone, so I floated the idea of putting the boys in with her for company. Katie had hardly been to the farm since Rio's death as she couldn't face seeing her empty stable, but eventually she was persuaded to come along and see Humbug, and oversee the experiment to put them all together.

We put the boys in with Spirit one sunny afternoon...but wouldn't be trying it again! Spirit flew into full dragon-mode as she chased them around, neck stretched, teeth bared...and they ran for their lives! It was the most exercise they'd had, or Spirit for that matter, in a while, and they were panting heavily, eyes wide, and nostrils flaring as they finally came to a trembling halt and hid behind Katie, peering cautiously through her legs while I restrained a furious Spirit!

It was the first time I'd seen Katie laugh in such a long time and it was like a tonic to us all. Rio's death had hit her harder than even I would have ever thought, but laughing at the ponies running like the clappers away from Spirit lightened everyone's mood, and even Spirit started to look a little happier.

Just a few short months later, in November 2019, Katie graduated from university. It was with enormous pride that I whooped and cheered as she walked in her gown, her very expensive dress, and beautiful red shoes across the stage of the City Hall in Sheffield to receive her certificate. She'd overcome so much over the 4 years of studying to reach this culmination of hard work, dedication, and commitment, and fully deserved the applause that rang around the audience.

I have absolutely no doubt that I was the proudest mum there, and despite the torrential rain that threatened to ruin our happy occasion, we posed for family photographs and later drank maybe one too many toasts to everything that had happened during those 4 years.

Our horsey family stayed at this hilly little farm for a couple of years, but then due to Joan's messy divorce from her husband, the place went up for sale. We'd seen this decision coming for a while, so it came as no surprise when it was suggested that we find somewhere else for Spirit and the boys, but again, we were in a position where we rang horsey friends, trawled social media sites, and rang local farmers; all of which resulted in nothing.

Then, as our leaving date was looming ever closer, I happened to join a local group on Facebook, where I saw an advert for a brand-new livery yard that would soon be opening up on a nearby dairy farm…large flat, lush fields, and it was within easy walking distance of home! I rang and arranged to go for a look, and it was on a miserable, rainy afternoon that Katie and I sloshed in our wellies through a fragrant mix of rainwater puddles and cowpat puddles in a typical Yorkshire dairy farmyard.

We rounded the corner opposite a barn full of curious cows twitching their shiny wet noses at us and found ourselves looking into a brand-new Dutch barn, very similar to the one at the equestrian centre from a few years ago. Smart, new internal stables beckoned and the promise of being able to walk there in winter (and stroll pleasantly in summer!) was a big draw. We arranged to move the following week!

Our yard owner, Joan, who over the couple of years that we'd been there had become a good friend, offered to transport the ponies and all of our belongings, which we packed up again with heavy hearts. We'd endured heartbreak and frustration, enjoyed fun and laughter, not to mention a few glasses of wine while at this hilly little yard; it was steep, muddy, rough and ready; the stables were, if I'm honest, a little shabby and, in heavy rain, a bit leaky, but I would miss it.

The new yard was only a couple of miles away, so Katie tacked Spirit up and rode her there, but it was a long trek for elderly, short Shetland legs, so the boys were happy to hitch a ride in Joan's trailer. The journey took less than 10 minutes, but by the time we arrived, Humbug had removed his headcollar, fiddled with (and somehow jammed) the lock for the groom's door, and bitten a hole in the haynet she left in there for her own horse! All very typical Humbug, really, and despite the frustration he causes, we love him for it!

Even Joan reluctantly agreed that despite being terrified of him, and him exploiting this by biting her at every opportunity, she would 'kind of' miss him.

Within hours of the move, Humbug had broken the automatic water drinker in their brand-new stable. He'd stuck his nose under a flap covering the filler and levelling mechanism, pulled out the plastic ballcock, and chewed it into pieces. Thankfully, we were still around, putting away our belongings in the ancient, spooky grain loft we'd been allocated for storage when we heard a splash and the gentle trickle of running water.

We knew that without a doubt Humbug would be involved and we ran back to the barn to find Toby standing wide-eyed on tip-hooves in the middle of the brand-new shavings bed, while Humbug delightedly pawed at the gathering pool at his feet!

We discovered in the very early days at our new yard, that the farmer had no experience of horses at all! The barn at the time was without lights or power sockets and the farmer was mystified that we wanted both.

"Watsa need 'lectrics foh, t'osses cn see int' dark!" (Roughly translated as: Why would I provide expensive lights and electricity for you to muck out after dark when it'd cost me nothing for you to do it in daylight?)

We patiently explained that in the winter months, horses will need to be brought in after a day in the field, checked over, groomed, rugged up, fed, etc., and as it goes dark by mid-afternoon when most of us are still at work, we'd quite like to be able to do this without needing head-torches. He wasn't convinced but, eventually, was persuaded that if he wanted his barn full of horses, the owners of which he was planning to relieve of considerable amounts of cash every month, he would need to provide what we assured him were the very basics.

He was fascinated to learn that we muck out every day. He mucks out his barns once a year when his cows are turned out into the field for the summer months. He'd stand shaking his head in disbelief as we slithered through the frozen yard with a loaded wheelbarrow, full of wet and dirty bedding to dump on the muckheap. He did capitalise on this though, as he realised what we were throwing out would be great to bed his cows down on, with just a sprinkle of straw over the top!

He had even less experience with Shetland ponies ('them there little 'osses'). We made a small paddock from our electric fencing and the farmer was fascinated to learn about the escapes Humbug has staged over the years. He later admitted to thinking we were wildly exaggerating, until one day, he looked out of his kitchen window, the farmhouse being several fields away, and saw Humbug and Toby standing side by side, peering back at him over the garden wall!

Instead of ringing us and have us return them to their small, suitably eaten-off paddock, he decided the poor starving boys would enjoy eating some lovely lush grass for a change and left them to it. They were out stuffing their faces for much of the day, but thankfully, were so engrossed in the prohibited grass that they didn't spot the narrow gap in the wall that leads into a housing estate! Another owner who'd brought her horse to live there a couple of weeks after us spotted that the paddock was empty and mercifully went searching for the escapees.

She said they were so full, that they could hardly waddle back across the fields to the stable and stood in a grass-filled stupor once she'd shut the door on them. Humbug was ok, thankfully, but due to the excess of vegetation, Toby had a touch of 'the squirts', which necessitated his bum needing to be washed later that evening, much to his mortification.

Apart from a few minor teething issues where it has become clear that the difference between dairy farmers and overly cautious horse owners turns out to be huge, we've struck up a good working relationship with the typical Yorkshire farmer and his family. 'Mr Farmer' is highly amused to see us washing our wellies of cow muck before getting into our otherwise clean cars and was mystified to learn that we clip and then rug our horses up against the harsh winter weather.

He was baffled as to why we spend a small fortune on feed and hay when there's a field full of grass right outside the door. Having said that, he is very quick to tell us on rainy winter days that the horses have to stay indoors, rather than muddy up his grass. This has caused a few heated arguments; bearing in mind most of us owners have jobs to go to, we arrive with time to feed, rug, and turn out our horses, whereas when at the last moment he makes a decision for them to be indoors for the day, we also have time-consuming mucking-out to do, water buckets to fill, and filled haynets to provide.

Persuading him that we needed an outdoor arena was tricky "There's miles and miles of roads for you to ride on, why do I need to dig up a field so you can ponce around and jump over things?"

He did, eventually, provide us with a very well-made outdoor arena, but drew the line at making showjumps for us. Those we've had to provide ourselves and it was a bizarre conversation that had me scratching my head when he flatly refused to let us paint the wings in bright colours.

35

Heartbreak, Happier Times and Beyond

We can never truly own a horse, but the special ones will always own a piece of our heart.
Lisa J. Gilbert

At the time of finishing the greater part of this story, Humbug is 25 and Toby is 20. Spirit, heartbreakingly, is no longer with us; the grand old lady, my 'heart horse', passed away 18 months ago as peacefully as I could hope for after a short illness at the age of 28. As I whispered my final goodbye into her ear on a cold, rainy March evening, I thought of all that she'd brought to me and my children. She truly was a family horse and I'll be forever in her debt for the love and the memories.

Her death affected me even more than I could have expected. She was such a massive part of my life for nearly 25 years; she'd been a constant and much-appreciated sanctuary of calm throughout the stresses of bringing up the children alone after my divorce from their father, she'd been there as a much-needed shoulder to cry on through those inevitable struggles, and I'd also been at my happiest during the years she'd been with me too. The grief is still very much at the surface.

Friends I've made at the yard stayed to support me, at a respectful distance, while she was gently put to sleep in the outdoor arena and afterwards allowed me time with her to cry and stroke her beautiful face before, out of my earshot, they phoned the local disposal company.

Unless you have copious amounts of your own land and machinery to dig enormous graves, there's no easy way of disposing of a horse's body, but the unceremonious winching of your beloved horse onto the lorry for its final journey is something I would suggest owners don't witness. Thankfully, my friends were there to oversee this awful task, and I'll always be grateful.

There's a newish member of our horsey family who came to us during the pandemic; a chunky little Welsh Cob called Taz! He's chock-full of personality, with a cheery disposition and a permanent smile on his face, so he fits in well. His arrival was an interesting occasion though; Katie had been thinking of buying a new horse and the pandemic provided her with loads of unexpected time on her hands due to the temporary closure of the restaurant she then managed. We trawled internet adverts and quickly realised that horses were going for premium prices!

Suddenly, everyone who'd ever wanted a horse found they had plenty of time to ride which they hadn't previously known, and sellers of horses took the maximum advantage of this. We were dismayed to see very ordinary horses with not much to shout about being advertised for ridiculously high prices. We were lamenting this fact to an owner at our yard, a delightful retired vicar, who could turn out some appalling language when her horse stood on her foot!

She thoughtfully suggested that we leave it with her as she 'might know of something'. A couple of days later, she gave us the phone number of a lady who had recently bought a youngster to take hunting and didn't really have the time to devote to the existing pony who'd originally been bought several years ago for her now adult daughter. Katie phoned her and we arranged to take a look the following weekend, having been surprised at the very reasonable price the owner was asking.

Our first look at Taz wasn't particularly inspiring; he simply looked like a bored little brown horse tied to the side of a stable on a smallholding. He was also quite a bit older than Katie had hoped but she agreed to try him on a hack, mainly out of politeness, while Annie and I waited for her in the car, expecting to drive her home again after half an hour to keep on looking. She arrived back an hour later with a huge smile on her face!

"He's fantastic!" She beamed. "He's bombproof in traffic, even with tractors and motorbikes; he's polite and well-mannered on a canter through the woods (i.e., he had brakes) and he splashed happily through a deep river, jumping like a stag up onto the banking on the other side!"

Suddenly, she'd made arrangements to ride him the 11 miles home the following day! The owner agreed to ride with her on the youngster she'd bought as she thought it'd be good experience for him, and by doing so, she'd get to have a look at where Taz would be living. She arranged for someone to pick her up from our place to take her and the young horse home again as she felt a 22-mile round trip was maybe a step (or two) too far!

It was a bright sunny day at the end of February when, after a pleasant, uneventful hack, Katie and her new bestie (don't tell Humbug I called him that!) along with the owner on her lovely, leggy grey youngster, Patrick, clip-clopped into the yard. Taz was looking around clearly interested in his new surroundings, and his 5-year-old pal was nearly on his knees! It was a good job transport home had been arranged for them!

The owner put the youngster in an empty stable with a full haynet and buckets of water, and Katie set about dismounting from Taz in order to untack him and put him into his new stable. This is where things went a tad pear-shaped! Taz, it turned out, was not used to being indoors and he panicked, being unable to see his friend who was by now stretched out on the bed already snoring. He set off for the barn gates at a gallop, still tacked up in saddle and bridle.

Katie tried heroically to hang on to his reins but she had little chance of stopping him. Shouts of 'GATE!' were too late and we watched in dismay as Taz's apple-shaped bum disappeared at speed through the gates and away! He had no idea of where he was, only where he'd come from, and we could hear him galloping up the road back in the direction of

229

where he knew was home. Hearts in mouths, a wide-eyed Annie, Katie as pale as I'd ever seen anyone, the owner who was muttering unprintable expletives, and I, all set off in my car to give chase.

Hikers and dog walkers kept trying to flag us down, warning us that there was a loose horse galloping amongst the traffic on the top side of the farm, heading at speed into the next village! Finally, we caught sight of Taz; he'd found himself face to face with a local farmer coming the other way on his tractor and sensibly Taz had turned around. He was now speed-trotting, nostrils flaring, back towards us, so Katie and the owner leapt out of the car to grab his reins which were by now tangled around his front legs.

He deftly sidestepped both of them and carried on going, but thankfully, in the direction of the yard. I turned the car around and followed him at a distance so as not to spook him, and I was unbelievably relieved when he was forced into turning into the yard by a car coming up the hill, its driver astonished at finding himself looking at a riderless horse taking itself on a hack.

Taz suddenly recognised where he was, walked calmly into the barn, parked himself outside the stable where his friend was still sleeping and had missed all the fun, and waited for us to catch up. Katie burst into relieved tears, her knees buckling from the rush of adrenaline, and Taz nudged her pockets, hoping for carrots! Yep—he fits in well!

36
The Final Chapter... Or Is It?

When you're young and you fall off a horse, you may break
something. When you're my age, you splatter!
Roy Rodgers

Technically, Taz belongs to Katie, but just 6 months after she bought him, she was offered her absolute dream job and, much to Humbug's dismay, moved 200 miles away. She'd had a wonderful summer of exploring the miles and miles of our beautiful Yorkshire countryside, getting to know Taz, and riding with friends to the local pub—the same one we bought lunch in after agreeing to buy Humbug. (If the landlord is reading, she's sorry about Taz knocking down the wall during a massive strop about being denied crisps!)

In those few months with, thanks to the pandemic, little to do but ride, she made some wonderful horsey memories to take with her to her new life. The agreement was that she'd drive back home every other weekend or so to ride, cuddle Humbug and have her horsey fix, and in between, I'd ride Taz to keep him fit and happy. I grumbled at the time about the responsibility, the extra burden, etc., but to be honest, I love it! He's a lot of fun; a charismatic little bundle of energy and he keeps me entertained with his 'extra' personality.

He and Humbug have a strange relationship, apparently based on mutual jealousy. Humbug is and always will be Katie's main man, but Taz feels that he also should be first in line for her affection on her weekends at home. It's a power struggle I'm afraid Taz simply isn't going to win while-ever Humbug draws breath!

Taz was a showjumper in a former home, quite successful we gather, and he occasionally jumps into the pony paddock purely for the fun of chasing Humbug and Toby around. Humbug is very creaky these days, with a front leg slightly misshapen due to his arthritis, but boy can he run when there's 450 kg of chunky Welsh Cob bearing down on him at speed! Taz will then jump back out and carry on with his day, grazing with the other horses in the field, and lazily whisking his tail against the flies.

Humbug is now on daily medication for his arthritis and has, in recent years, been diagnosed with Cushing's syndrome; so far he doesn't need medication for this and the only outward sign is that his hair grows thick and fast. Thankfully, he's happy to be clipped, so we keep him comfortable by keeping his hair short; it's also much easier to wash off the mud!

It was during Katie's university years that I had the idea of writing Humbug's memoirs. I'd half-heartedly started a Twitter account of my own a couple of years earlier, but soon it became a forum for detailing what the little troublemaker had been up to during the day, and the account was soon transferred from being mine to being a daily account of Humbug's adventures, written 'by' Humbug himself.

He quickly gained far more followers than I had done and I soon discovered that other people were as daft as me, with their horses, pigs, cats, dogs, guinea pigs, and rabbits chatting away to 'Humbug' like old pals! This was the perfect forum for me to decide whether there was enough interest in Humbug and Toby's day-to-day adventures for me to consider writing them down, which I often did on the backs of envelopes when inspiration struck, with a view to publishing at some point. This brings us neatly to you, having hopefully enjoyed what I've written so far!

There have been a few bits of the story that didn't make it into here: Humbug letting himself into the kitchen of the farmhouse and eating not only the entire contents of the fruit-bowl, but also a box of Weetabix, and a bag of flour, is one tale, although absolutely true, that simply sounded too unlikely, even for Humbug!

And the time he escaped from his field, ended up in the farmyard, and ate all the trailing pink geraniums in the previously very decorative hanging baskets…which wouldn't have been too disastrous, had they not been painstakingly and tenderly nurtured by our lovely surrogate mum, Glenda, and planted especially to be included in the photos of a forthcoming family wedding!

And the time a very drunk Fran (possibly to win a bet) rode him bareback through an increasingly raucous summer barbeque; Humbug grabbed a burnt sausage on the way past and, amid cries of 'he's supposed to be a vegetarian!', thoroughly enjoyed his impromptu snack!

And the time he escaped into the farm's walled garden, shimmied under the side of the poly-tunnel, and ate all the baby carrots! He was later found in a complete food coma by the farmer, who after prodding his ample backside with a booted toe, stated that he 'Thot it wor deed'. (Presumably, this meant the farmer thought Humbug had succumbed to the excess of carrots and had met his maker!)

And the time we couldn't find him anywhere during a heavy rainfall until we realised a friend's cob had mysteriously grown an extra four legs. We realised Humbug was standing completely underneath Pops, using him as a very effective shelter from the rain!

And the semi-serious conversation Katie and I had years ago when we wondered if he could be smartened up enough to pull a Cinderella-style carriage taking her and a couple of pals the last mile or so to her Y11 Prom. Knowing him as you do now, can you imagine the carnage he could have caused? I can't believe we considered it even for a moment!

Hopefully, there are a few more stories in him yet that can be included in the next book, assuming Humbug remains his charming, charismatic, irritating, infuriating, hilarious self!

Thank you so much for reading. I hope you enjoyed reading it as much as I enjoyed writing it!

Humbug would like to invite you to follow him on what used to be Twitter and is now the unfortunately named 'X'; @HumbugAndToby. He updates pretty much daily, which considering he doesn't have thumbs, is quite a task! He posts photographs and videos and is happy to boast of his exploits, be it biting me on the leg, escaping from his paddock, his stable, the arena, or anywhere else that we try to contain him. He occasionally allows Toby and Taz to feature in his tweets and looks forward to welcoming you there!

He has also started an Instagram account, humbug_and_toby, and a Bluesky account, @humbugandtoby.bsky.social and promises to update regularly!

Humbug's Favourite
Flapjack Recipe

Ingredients:

- 3 large carrots, grated
- 2 large apples, grated
- 2 tablespoons vegetable oil
- ¼ mug molasses (or half a mug if you're a greedy Shetland pony)
- 1 teaspoon salt
- 1 mug oats
- 1 mug of your regular horse feed
- Polo mints to decorate

Method:

- Ask your human to set the oven to 180 degrees C.
- In a large bowl, mix the carrots, apples, oil, and molasses (yum!) until combined.
- Add the oats, salt, and your feed and stir again until all ingredients are combined. It will be sticky and dough-like; add a bit of flour if it sticks too much to your hooves.

- Form into small rounds (approx. 1" balls) with your hooves, or you could ask your human to use their hands.
- Place the rounds on a baking tray and bake for around 25/30 minutes until they're a lovely golden brown (a bit like Toby).
- While the flapjack rounds are still warm, decorate each one with a Polo mint.
- Allow to cool, and enjoy!

(Don't forget to lick out the bowl!)

These delicious morsels have made great Christmas gifts for some of our pals at the yard; ask your human to pop a few into fancy bags and tie them with a Christmassy ribbon!